How to Turn
YOUR WORDS
into Money

Also by Emerson & Church

The Fundraiser's Guide to Irresistible Communications, by Jeff Brooks, 143 pp., $24.95.

Here it is: an easy-to-read and spritely book that reveals what really works in fundraising. Not academic theory or wishful thinking, but ways of communicating that are proven to motivate donors to give generously, wholeheartedly, and repeatedly.

Drawing from decades of in-the-trenches experience, Jeff Brooks, one of America's top fundraising writers, takes you on a step-by-step tour of the unique strategies, writing style, and design techniques of irresistible fundraising messages.

How to Write Fundraising Materials that Raise More Money, by Tom Ahern, 187 pp., $24.95.

Whenever we're called upon to draft a solicitation letter, or write copy for the website, or, heaven forbid, pen long stretches of a proposal or case statement, we sit there … and if we're lucky crank out serviceable prose. Few would call it sparkling. Even fewer are moved to write a check in response.

It won't be this way any longer for those who invest a few hours in *How to Write Fundraising Materials that Raise More Money*. Communicating with donors is the bedrock of all fundraising. And no book addresses this topic with such virtuosity.

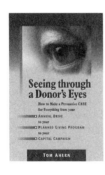

Seeing Through a Donor's Eyes, by Tom Ahern, 167 pp., $24.95.

Successful donor newsletters, websites, annual reports, donor acquistion programs, email, direct mail, and, yes, capital campaigns, too, all have one thing in common: behind each stands a well-reasoned, emotionally satisfying case for support.

Regularly reviewing your case is mere due diligence in a well-managed fundraising office. And it doesn't have to be a laborious project, either: answer three questions and you can be done.

Of course, if your office is launching a big-bucks campaign, the step-by-step process revealed in this book guarantees you'll tell a persuasive, sharply focused story, even when you have a thousand moving parts.

www.emersonandchurch.com

How to Turn YOUR WORDS into Money

The Master Fundraiser's Guide to Persuasive Writing

JEFF BROOKS

Emerson
& Church
PUBLISHERS

First printed in September 2015

Printed in the United States of America
This text is printed on acid-free paper.

Copies of this book are available from the publisher at discount when purchased in quantity.

Library of Congress Cataloging-in-Publication Data

Brooks, Jeff, 1961–
    How to turn your words into money : the master fundraiser's guide to persuasive writing / Jeff Brooks.
      pages   cm
      ISBN 978-1-889102-55-9 (pbk. : alk. paper)   1. Fund raising. 2. Persuasion (Rhetoric) 3. Proposal writing for grants. 4. Nonprofit organizations—Marketing.   I. Title.
      HV41.2.B7623 2015
      658.15'224—dc23
      2015020229

Emerson & Church, Publishers
15 Brook Street, Medfield, MA 02052
Tel. 508-359-0019
www.emersonandchurch.com

Contents

Foreword   7

Introduction   9

I   The Style of Fundraising Writing

1   Four Things That Don't Work in Fundraising   15

2   Fundraising Writing Is Different   31

3   Be SURE about Your Writing   47

4   The Call to Action   57

5   The Magic Words   65

6   The Sound of Your Writing   71

II   Why Stories Matter in Fundraising

7   The Elements of a Well-Built Story   79

8   Five Ways to Use Stories for Impact   89

9   How Storytellers Tell Stories   97

10   The Hero of the Story   103

11   Word Pictures   111

III   What We're Really Doing: The Psychology of Fundraising

12   The Evil Cousin of Fundraising   121

13   Wholehearted Fundraising: Meeting Donors'
     Emotional Needs   129

14   What Good Is Guilt?   137

15   Four Smart Assumptions about Donors   141

IV   A Brief Survival Guide

16   Who's Ready for the Ahern Rule?   151

17   Five Fundraising Traps and How to Avoid Them   155

18   Things I Wish I'd Learned Sooner   165

Foreword

Okay, I admit it. I got hooked on *How to Turn Your Words into Money*.

From the very first page, I started underlining, making check marks, writing in the margins, circling paragraphs. By the time I finished the book, every page looked like a road map of New Jersey.

Jeff's book is filled with wisdom, along with a generous sprinkling of wit. You'll find gems on every page. In fact, every page is a lesson you can put to use.

Here's what's best of all. Whether you're writing copy for a direct mail piece, a letter requesting a grant, or writing a case statement, *How to Turn Your Words into Money* is written as if it's meant just for you.

Jeff writes about the magic word. THE magic word. I won't give it away. You'll have to read the book.

And then there's the section on freewriting. For anyone who puts pen to paper, this alone is worth the price of the book. And the "Survival Guide." And the "Ahern Rule."

There's something else. There are dozens of examples of poor, dull writing that Jeff rewrites to show you how to make your words exciting and compelling. I personally think this is the best way to learn.

It really hit home for me when Jeff wrote that the fundraising story must not end with the problem solved. Bingo! "It should end unsolved, a cliffhanger, waiting for the donor to take action."

If someone does a book on effective writing, you would expect it to be well-written. Jeff is insanely effective. He writes from the head to the heart.

I loved the book. You will, too.

Jerold Panas

What Are We Doing Here?

Who *chooses* to become a fundraising writer? And why? It's never been romanticized in the movies. The money isn't exactly bountiful. Most people aren't even aware that fundraising requires the work of professionals. They seem to think it just seeps out of nonprofit organizations, some kind of natural by-product.

I'll tell you how I got here: I was hoodwinked.

My first "real" job after college was with a small nonprofit supporting humanitarian work in India. My duty: to write and edit the organization's monthly newsletter. I figured it would be a cool way to spend a few years before going to graduate school.

"By the way," the new boss told me on my first day, "you'll be writing some *other materials* besides the newsletter." I failed to note the vocal italics he put on *other materials*. Rookie mistake.

The other materials turned out to be direct mail fundraising—a lot of it.

Like many people in their twenties, I didn't grasp the psychology of fundraising. The conventions of direct mail seemed stupid. The whole exercise was opaque to my imagination and baffling to my intellect. Every fundraising assignment felt like a slog through quicksand against an incoming tide.

At that time, we didn't have the resources available now. The foundational books on fundraising by Mal Warwick, Jerold Panas, Tom Ahern, and others had yet to be written. Blogs and webinars didn't exist. There were few conferences for fundraisers, and my little organization couldn't afford to send me anyway.

I was on my own. Until I found a book titled *Dear Friend: Mastering the Art of Direct Mail Fund Raising*, by the late Kay Partney Lautman. I studied that big yellow book like it was Scripture.

I left the job just as I was starting to understand fundraising. I spent the next few years nosing my way around the academic maze before realizing that wasn't where I wanted to spend the rest of my career. So I found my way back to fundraising. That was more than twenty-five years ago.

A lot of us end up writing fundraising by accident or under false pretenses. This oddball orphan of a career seems to have a way of ensnaring people who intended to do something else. It's a good thing, too.

However you ended up as a fundraising writer, on purpose or not, I hope you know how important you are.

Writers are the Marine Corps of the fundraising world. Not the fanciest or the best funded, but the ones who get the job done—even when it seems impossible.

We start with an organization's need for revenue. We end up with a written synthesis of why the cause is worth supporting. We capture the soul of the relationship between a nonprofit and its donors. You might even say we create the relationship.

Sometimes it seems like alchemy. But you know what it really is: It's just work. You hold half a dozen clashing precepts in your mind. You follow counterintuitive truths that most people don't believe. Then you write, rewrite, and rewrite again until it sings.

This book is about the theory and practice of writing effective fundraising materials. I've focused especially on the things that make fundraising writing different from other disciplines. We'll spend some time creeping in the deep weeds. Sometimes we'll rise above it all like toga-wearing philosophers exploring Eternal Truths.

My hope is this book will help you become better equipped, more enthusiastic, and empowered to win battles with those who don't get it. But most of all, I hope it helps you raise truckloads of money to support good work.

Here's to good writing for good deeds!

PART I

The Style of Fundraising Writing

Once upon a time, I was an English teacher. A guardian and promoter of our written language.

It has come back to bite me many times.

I worked hard to teach my students specific rules about writing. At the time, it seemed like an uphill battle, even a hopeless cause. But some students were paying attention. Who knew?

Some now work at nonprofit organizations. And they're repeating the things I used to say.

The problem is most of those rules I taught don't belong in fundraising.

These former students are telling me I shouldn't use informal language. That my sentence fragments are sloppy, my colloquial grammar an abomination. They want fundraising that's less repetitive, more concise, with smoother transitions. With longer paragraphs, each starting with a topic sentence. They believe my fundraising is defective if I start a sentence with a conjunction, split an infinitive, or use a cliché. Some of them even take their red pens to contractions. (Honest—I never told anyone to avoid contractions!)

Call it karma. I'm just getting served up what I dished out.

The trouble is fundraising writing owes little to the rules we learned in English class. It has a specific obligation to motivate donors to give. And that means a different set of rules.

I'm not suggesting we forget everything English teachers said. They taught us how to write with vigor and precision. They showed us how using language helps marshal our thoughts. And they made us believe in revising our work.

But if your job is fundraising, your goal isn't to please a former instructor. It's to get people to look past their self-interest, to tap into their inner angels and join you in changing the world. That's a tall order. It's much trickier than pulling down an A in English Lit. And it requires a different approach to writing.

In this first section, we'll spend time on the unique conventions of fundraising writing. We'll explore how it differs from other types of writing, and we'll discuss the techniques that lead to success.

We'll start by looking at some common approaches that don't work. Then we'll look at some that do. Finally, we'll dive into the details of how to write messages designed to motivate giving.

Consider this a sort of atonement for me. If I can help you fight back the "proper" rules I used to promote, I'll be one step closer to redemption.

CHAPTER 1

Four Things That Don't Work in Fundraising

You might think musicians who play string instruments don't have to worry about breathing. If only. I play a string instrument, and I'm sorry to report there's a lot more to it than knowing exactly where to place your fingers.

During difficult passages, many players do something dumb: They hold their breath. It feels like the right thing to do, but it undermines your ability to play, especially the hard stuff. Your muscles and tendons get tight. Your movements lose fluidity and control. You play like a rusty robot. It's no fun, it hurts, and you sound awful.

I'm telling you this because something similar happens to fundraising writers.

Some approaches that instinctively seem right—aren't. Until you learn otherwise, you'll gravitate to one or more of them. I'm going to show you four of the common (and tempting) "hold-your-breath" approaches to fundraising.

I'm not thrilled to tell you how I know they don't work. . . . I know because I've done them all. I'll even try them again, I bet. That's how tempting they are. *It'll be different this time,* I'll tell myself.

But I'm hoping I can spare you the trouble. Help you spend less time holding your breath and struggling. Maybe then you'll devote more time connecting with donors in ways that motivate them to give.

1. Educating Is Not Fundraising

How many times have you heard someone say that to raise funds we must "educate the donors"?

Every time someone tries to do that, truckloads of #10 envelopes are dumped into landfills unopened.

The sad truth is, educating donors isn't compatible with motivating them to give. Worse yet, it isn't an achievable goal. When you try to educate people into giving, they don't give. And they don't become more educated.

There's a simple reason why: Most people, most of the time, have no interest in becoming more educated.

I saw this in action when I was a teacher. The coolest thing I could do for my students—something that would literally stir them to applause—was to cancel a class. To tell them in effect, "Tomorrow, you won't get your education. It's what you've dedicated this period of your life to. It's costing you (or someone) a pile of money. But it's cancelled. See you Monday."

It's not just college students, either. Just about everyone flees from attempts to become educated. We consider learning a fine ideal but something to avoid.

There's one major exception. And that exception matters a great deal to fundraisers. Nearly everyone has interests they pursue with passion.

Among my friends, there's one who's highly educated about Thai cooking. Another is into church vestments, while a third is interested in the history of golf. These friends seek information about their passions. They read about them, follow blogs, visit websites, and "like" these topics on Facebook. They even take classes.

But you're wasting your time, and theirs, if you try to hammer into them something they don't care about.

In other words, what's relevant, interesting, and worthwhile comes from within.

In childhood we're forced to learn what adults decide is important. After that, each of us sets our own learning agenda. Somebody else's idea of what we should learn blows past us like a light breeze.

In your mind, your organization's cause is one of the most important issues facing the people of Planet Earth. To almost everyone else, it's a distraction from much more interesting topics, like, say, the history of golf.

Here's an example of fundraising that tries to educate donors into giving:

```
You might not know this, but the typical
homeless person in our area is not the
bearded elderly man who just needs a hot
meal. Forget that stereotype! Less than 10
```

```
percent of our clients are over the age of
sixty.
     Far more typical is the young mother with
a couple of children in tow.
     They don't just need meals. They need
holistic services to help them overcome the
root causes of the problems that landed them
on the street.
```

The lecturing tone of the example isn't accidental. When we try to instruct, we tend to imitate teachers, and not just the good ones. We often communicate that tone of weary annoyance. We might as well make that wah-wah-wah trumpet sound that signifies adults talking on the old Charlie Brown specials.

Still, suppose your lecture gets through and succeeds in changing someone's view about who is homeless and what we need to do about it. Congratulations. But you still don't have a donation.

People give for emotional reasons, not because of facts they accumulate. That's why you raise a lot more money by writing like this:

```
Life has been hard on Karl. He served in
the first Gulf War, and he's never quite come
home from the front lines. He lives under
one end of the 13th Street Bridge. He's been
```

```
there a few years—Karl doesn't know how
long.
    Karl's rugged face is covered with scars.
He always has new injuries. It's not from the
war. Karl gets mugged every few weeks. Not
because anyone would think he has money, but
because he looks like he won't fight back.
Which he doesn't.
```

This passage isn't about homelessness. It's about Karl. It doesn't paint the Big Picture. It paints a small picture of one person.

People love reading about people. And when you touch their hearts by telling them about a person, they're much more likely to give.

Here's the wonderful part. When a donor makes a gift, she'll care more about your cause. The more she cares, the more interested she'll be in learning about it. That makes her a better donor, and a better advocate, volunteer, thinker, voter, and prayer. She'll even become a more complete human being.

In other words, when you motivate someone to give, you set a virtuous cycle in motion. Giving leads to knowledge. Knowledge leads to giving.

On the other hand, when you try to educate, you set nothing in motion. No giving, no increased knowledge either.

There's a Zen saying: *When the pupil is ready, the teacher appears.* It's up to us fundraisers to appear when donors are ready, and leave them be when they aren't.

2. Bragging Is Not Fundraising

Let's look at two scenarios for the beginning of a relationship.

Scenario 1

> Boy: Hey, I noticed you aren't eating the eggplant Parmesan.
> Girl: I don't care much for eggplant.
> Boy: No kidding! I hate eggplant, too!
> Girl tells an anecdote about how her dislike for eggplant nearly caused her to lose her job.

This relationship has potential. The pair starts with what they have in common and builds from there.

Scenario 2

> Boy: I'm not eating the eggplant Parmesan. I have hated eggplant since 1982, and I hate it 12 percent more than anyone else in my demographic. I also hate rutabagas, okra, and parsnips. My disdain isn't confined to vegetables. I hate goat's milk, grits, pork, scallops, and blancmange. You might call me the most cutting-edge, efficient hater in the U.S.
> Girl excuses herself, starts running as soon as she's out of sight.

That relationship doesn't stand a chance. Because Boy is working from the wrongheaded assumption that if he can show his excellence with enough force, he'll win Girl over. He hasn't learned there's little chance for a relationship when you make the conversation all about yourself.

Everyone knows this. Yet many organizations approach fundraising just that way. If we impress people enough, show them exactly how awesome we are, they'll flock to our side with undying loyalty and gobs of revenue.

It doesn't work in fundraising any better than in other aspects of life.

The temptation to brag is strong. After all, you need to show donors your organization is worth their consideration. That their gifts will have impact. But the trick is to show donors the information they need, without the chest-thumping. Here are two ways to do that:

Only share excellent qualities that are relevant to donors.

Many of your qualities are uninteresting and unimportant to donors. Talking about them because they're important to you is bragging. I mean things like these:

- ▶ *Your excellent processes.* Donors don't give to fund processes. They give to produce results, outcomes. (More about this later.)
- ▶ *Awards you've won.* Congratulations. But unless it's a Nobel Prize, it's not meaningful outside your profession.
- ▶ *The fame of your president or other leaders.* Is there anything more off-putting than being told someone you've never heard of is famous? Fame speaks for itself.

Make the donor part of the narrative about your excellence.

The reason your excellence matters is because it increases the donor's impact. In fundraising that means: Don't just say you're excellent, tell the donor how your excellence boosts the impact of his giving.

You might feel tempted to say something like this:

```
We've been working on Skid Row since 1932,
longer than any other social service pro-
vider. We've built state-of-the-art facili-
ties, and our staff are the best-trained and
most-advanced professionals in the commu-
nity, bar none!
```

Don't do that! It's bragging. Instead, turn those facts around so they're about the donor's impact.

```
People like you have been helping the lost
and hurting of Skid Row through us since
1932. Thanks to generous friends like you,
our new building is roomy and efficient—spe-
cifically designed to help as many people
as possible. We'll stretch every dollar you
give so you help the greatest number of
people in the most life-transforming way.
```

When you tell the story this way, you're in the donor's context, not yours.

There are some facts about your excellence that will help donors feel confident about their giving. You should make these things available to donors:

► Watchdog approvals or ratings.
► Quotes from appropriate celebrities or authorities who vouch for you.
► A purpose statement that speaks to donors and helps them to see that you share their values.

*   *   *

Don't think of your fundraising as recruiting donors into your army. It's more like *you're* applying to the donor to join *her* army. She has a goal, and you must show how your mission accomplishes her mission.

Journalism Is Not Fundraising

It's fitting that when Superman is off duty, he's a reporter. Journalists, as far as I'm concerned, are the super-persons of the writing world.

Studying journalism is a great way to make yourself a stronger, more useful writer. Journalism hones your ability to gather information, organize your writing, and make it clear. All while working under deadline.

But good journalism isn't good fundraising. If you apply all the virtues of the field to fundraising, you can expect weak results and disengaged donors.

The foundation of reporting the news is the five Ws: Who, What, Where, Why, and When, plus How. Answer these questions and you're on your way to quality reporting. But not quality fundraising.

It takes a few Ws to tell any story. But if you focus on the Ws only, you'll miss the most important element of the story: the donor.

Y is the critical letter in fundraising. *Y* means *You.*

Fundraising stories are not efficient accounts of events. They're aimed at the heart, not the head. Fundraising stories put the donor inside the story, make her feel it, not just know it.

Here's how you might tell the story of a local homeless man when you use the framework of journalism:

```
Frank Gorman [WHO] spent last Christmas
[WHAT & WHEN] under the 15th Avenue Bridge
[WHERE]. It was his only option. He'd spent
his last dollars buying gifts for the two
young daughters he hadn't seen in more than
two years [WHY].
```

That might be the way the local paper would tell the story. It's clear and factual. It gets right to the point. But it's not about the reader. It's just one of many stories about other people she'll read or hear on any given day.

Here's the same story, told in a donor-focused way:

```
Frank is a lot like you. He loves his kids,
and like you, he'd do almost anything to
make them happy. But last Christmas, Frank
had to make a bigger sacrifice than most
parents. . . .
```

This version has most of the journalistic Ws in it. But the important thing is it has the Y—you. This makes the story meander, but it helps make the tale part of a donor's life. And that's what it takes to motivate action.

But here's how the values of good journalism can *really* kill your fundraising: Journalism is objective. It doesn't take sides. It avoids even the appearance of slanting the facts to support a particular point of view. That's the right way to report the news. (I sure wish more news outlets actually stuck to this approach!)

Objectivity isn't appropriate in our field. When you become a fundraiser, you take sides, you're wildly biased. Your cause is too important for you to keep the distance of journalistic objectivity.

I was working for a religious international relief organization when I heard the following account. A village elder in a community where the nonprofit worked forbade people from killing the rats that were eating up stored crops. The elder claimed the rats were the result of a curse put on them by a ghost. Killing the rats, he claimed, would only bring down a more terrible curse. The result was high malnutrition among the children. The organization was working to persuade people to ignore his command.

It was a great story. It captured the ethos of the organization: how they fought poverty by dealing with root causes, including cultural and spiritual practices. I wanted to tell the story this way:

Witch Doctor's Reign of Terror Is Killing Children

A staff writer, a journalism major, said it was more appropriate to be even-handed and not take sides:

Traditional Shaman Struggles to Follow Cultural Practices of His Tribe

The latter may be the balanced, unbiased way to tell the story, if you're reporting it as news. But that's not how you tell the story to donors who have money in their hands and want to use it to do something that puts their values to work.

Objectivity turns what could be a powerful fundraising story into an inert account of events. It's just information. It might be interesting to some readers, but for most it's yet another story they can ignore.

To create well-told (and subjective) fundraising messages, do the things that work:

▶ *Seek the drama.* Focus on conflict, brokenness, or things that need to change.

▶ *Show a problem.* Don't just show situations. Your reader needs to know there's a problem before she'll want to be part of a solution.

▶ *Unveil the enemy.* Stories with enemies are always more interesting. Sometimes the enemy is a person. Sometimes it's a disease, a belief, or a bad situation. But always show donors the enemy they're fighting.

▶ *Recruit the reader.* Fundraising is about getting someone on board. Appeal to his values and beliefs. Challenge him to take the action he knows he should take.

These steps might get you fired from The Associated Press, but they're right for fundraising.

4. The Funny Thing about Humor

A TV newscaster in Australia gets a dream assignment: Interview the Dalai Lama. He decides to start the way he often does—by telling a joke to put his subject at ease. Unfortunately, he decides to tell the Dalai Lama a Dalai Lama joke. It goes something like this:

> "The Dalai Lama walks into a pizza joint and says, 'Can you make me one with everything?'"

His Holiness looks at the newscaster blankly. He asks an aide what pizza is.

The newscaster tries again, amplifying with hand motions.

The Dalai Lama has no idea that "one with everything" is a Western caricature of Buddhism. Nothing about the joke makes any sense to him.

Following an awkward silence—eons in TV-time—the Dalai Lama starts to giggle. But he's not laughing at the joke. He's chuckling at the newscaster's cartoonish discomfort.*

Humor doesn't travel well across cultural lines. What you intend as funny can be anything from meaningless to a gross insult for your audience. That's why humor isn't a good way to raise funds.

Understand, there's a cultural gap between you and your donors. It can be as wide as the gap between the hapless newscaster and the Dalai Lama. Actually, there are several gaps:

▶ You're an insider at your organization. The donor isn't. You know the culture, the beliefs, the shared knowledge, and the received wisdom. The donor is privy to none of this.

▶ No matter how well informed your donor may be, you know a lot more about your cause. Things that are obvious to the point of boring to you are likely surprising to your donor.

▶ You are younger. And humor-wise, that's about as uncrossable a chasm as there is. If you don't believe me, try telling your grandmother a joke.

---

* This is a true story. If you don't believe me, find it on YouTube. Warning: May induce severe cringing.

In my family, there's a type of story we call a "Grandpa Joke." It's deadpan wit of the type my father enjoyed telling my kids, always leaving them gaping and puzzled. Example: We'd be visiting Grandpa and, after calling for everyone's attention, he'd darkly announce, "Friday the 13th is on a Wednesday this month."

"Even Grandpa doesn't laugh at Grandpa Jokes," my daughter observed. I once saw him tell his own mother the Friday the 13th joke. She laughed out loud, despite having heard it nearly monthly for decades. But that joke had no chance with my kids. Sometimes I realize I'm telling a Grandpa Joke. The clue is when you see everyone start to disengage.

There's a more fundamental problem with humor that makes it bad for fundraising—even if your donors somehow get the joke. The psychological foundation of most humor is a sense of superiority—sometimes gentle, sometimes cruel, but always there. You're laughing at something or someone. You're pulling something over on them. This sense of superiority is about as far from the emotion that leads to charity as you can get.

When you use humor in your fundraising, you pollute the atmosphere. You make empathy and kindness difficult.

Being funny while fundraising is like belting out punk rock while soothing a baby to sleep. You could be good at both. But not at the same time.

*   *   *

We've been looking at some of the things fundraising is *not*. Next, we'll do something even more important: discover what good fundraising *is*.

CHAPTER 2

Fundraising Writing Is Different

If you want to see how different two writing styles can be, look at two giants of twentieth-century American fiction: Ernest Hemingway and William Faulkner.

These two geniuses probably never met, though they did trade some famous barbs.* Looking at their differences, it's no surprise. You'd think they lived on different planets.

Faulkner's writing is thick, slow, and saturated with ten-dollar words like *apotheosis*. His sentences are sometimes so long, the beginning fades like the morning mist by the time you make it to the end.

Hemingway's writing is clear, sharp, and simple. With those famously short sentences. And fragments. Staccato rhythm—small words strung like bullets on a bandolier.

---

* Hemingway said, "Poor Faulkner. Does he really think big emotions come from big words?"

You may prefer one of these authors over the other (I go with Faulkner). But you'd have to be thick headed to claim the one you like less was doing literature wrong.

They're simply different. They used different techniques to reach different goals.

If a Hemingway specialist critiqued Faulkner by saying his sentences are too long, he'd just be displaying his ignorance. If a Faulkner expert complained that Hemingway's plots move too fast, you'd know she was out to lunch.

Faulknerish Hemingway would be bad Hemingway. Hemingway-like Faulkner would be laughable.

Fundraising writing has a distinct style, too. It's as unlike other genres as Hemingway is from Faulkner. That's lost on many people when they encounter our work. They want to correct it. They try to make it like some type of writing they're more accustomed to.

Fundraising Style Is Colloquial

One of the cool things about being a writer is using words like *paint* to create multi-sensory scenes. It's almost magic:

> "The nozzles were variously set but usually so there was a long sweet stream of spray, the nozzle wet in the hand, the water trickling the right forearm and the peeled-back cuff, and the water whishing out a long loose and and the low-curved cone, and so gentle a sound."*

---

* From *A Death in the Family*, by James Agee, a wonderful book I highly recommend to everyone, especially writers.

Just because you can write that way doesn't mean you should. The writing in this example is superb, strong prose. But it wouldn't be good for raising money.

Fundraising should be written to sound the way people talk. Colloquial voice creates the welcome illusion that the printed word is a person talking.

Writing colloquially is a higher skill than multi-sensory scene painting. It requires a sharp ear. You need to be able to hear the rhythm of speech and master the syntax, which is so unlike that of written English.

The tricky part is if you merely copy real speech, it's unreadable. You have to find a compromise that captures the cadence and word choice of speech while being orderly enough to follow on the page.

Here are a few hallmarks of well-written, colloquial fundraising:

> ▶ *Simple, short sentences.* Most sentences in fundraising should be under ten words. Most should follow the standard subject/verb/object pattern: "The boy ate the rice." Not "The rice, having been eaten by the boy, was now gone." But of course you'll want to vary sentence length and structure.
>
> ▶ *Passive voice.* Most writing teachers would have you believe that passive voice is a deadly plutonium olive in your writing cocktail. Really, it's not that bad. Skillful writers use it when the action is more important than the doer: "Frank was arrested on Christmas Day." (Who needs to be told it was a police officer who arrested him?)

A string of passive sentences would be flabby and dull. But there's nothing wrong with using the passive voice occasionally.

▶ *Sentence fragments.* Anyone who tells you sentence fragments are improper and make you look stupid isn't paying attention to real life. In speech, we use fragments more often than complete sentences. Really.

▶ *Contractions.* Colloquial English is full of contractions. Many of them we avoid in print, like *when'll* and *there're.* Some like *I'll* or *he's* are so common that not using the contraction can change the sense of what you're saying. You sound angry (or like my high school Latin teacher) if you write, "I will see you later."

▶ *Easy words.* Many honestly believe that multisyllabic words are better than short words. As if big words carry more weight, dignity, or authority. They don't. They're just harder to read. Words like *acquire* (get), *alleviate* (fix), *employ* (use), *endeavor* (try), *facilitate* (help), *individual* (person), *utilize* (use) make your writing worse for your reader. Choose the smaller word most of the time.*

---

* "Never use a long word where a short one will do" (from George Orwell's classic 1946 essay on writing, "Politics and the English Language."

The Little Book That Could
Kill Your Writing Style

You probably had an English teacher who sang the praises of a little book titled *The Elements of Style*, often called "Strunk and White," after its authors.

If you were forced to buy this book, sell it. Free yourself from its clutches.

Strunk and White has more bad writing advice per page than almost any other book published.

Far too much of it is pointlessly bossy or just wrong. Like, "Do not inject opinion." Really? What genre would that be?

Perhaps Strunk and White's most damaging advice is "Use the active voice." As I mentioned before, the passive voice is the right choice in many situations.

Then there's the fact that the book so often fails to follow its own advice. In the section urging writers to "Put statements in positive form," you find this sentence: "The adjective hasn't been built that can pull a weak or inaccurate noun out of a tight place." That sentence has five violations: It's in negative form, uses passive voice, and has three adjectives. It's not a bad sentence. But you'd never write it if you follow Strunk and White. Which it seems Strunk and White knew better than to do.

Fundraising Style Isn't Afraid of Clichés

More than a few English teachers (along with George Orwell) seem to think it's better to commit a war crime than to use a cliché in your writing.

I beg to differ.

Ordinary folks—I mean everyone, including you and me—use clichés all the time. Clichés make communication easier because they don't force the listener to think. Most are metaphors that everyone knows. They work because they're vivid, but mostly because, well, people know 'em like the backs of their hands.

Fundraising Style Is Choppy

You may have spent years learning how to make transitions buttery smooth—with no abrupt topic switches. This is a mark of good style in many types of writing.

We don't have time for that in fundraising. We jerk abruptly from topic to topic, paying little attention to transitions.

That's because our readers skim over copy like dragonflies on a pond. If they alight on some transitional material that doesn't lead them to action, we stand a good chance of losing them. Far better to be choppy than to lose readers before they get the message!

Anyway, choppiness is more evident to us than it is to our readers. Tom Ahern brilliantly points out that you and I and the people who approve our copy read it slowly—creeping along at one mile an hour, noticing every bump and pothole with spine-compressing clarity. Our readers are traveling 100 mph—flying over the bumps without even realizing they're there.

Fundraising Style Is Easy to Read

There are two ways to make your copy easy to read: the writing itself, and the way it is arranged on the page. We pay attention to both, because easy reading is one of the key qualities of fundraising writing.

To make the writing readable, use short sentences and short words, as I suggested earlier. They combine to create a low reading grade level.

Low grade level doesn't mean uneducated. It just means your writing is easier to read and understand. Reading level isn't like the ski slopes—where downhill racers would be bored with the easy slopes. It's more like rush-hour traffic. Everyone, no matter how good they are at driving, prefers a light, easy commute.

Check your writing with a grade-level calculator. You can find them online and built into Word and other word-processing programs. If your writing is higher than sixth grade, you're probably not being clear. Or worse, you're losing readers. That includes the physicians, rocket scientists, and philologists among them.

As for making your writing visually easy, litter your copy with entry points. Places that catch a wandering reader and pull her into the flow of words:

- ► Short (and varied) paragraphs.
- ► Emphasis, such as underlining, highlighting, boldface, italic type, and other disruptions.
- ► Open space, like wide margins, space between paragraphs, even that extra space after a period. And indent paragraphs. That helps readability, too.
- ► Subheads, margin notes, and other visual entry points.

These things make the page look messy. That's okay. It's more than okay, it's excellent. More people will read it.

Fundraising Style Is Long

I know length of message isn't a style attribute, but it's a winner in fundraising copy. Long messages almost always work better than short ones.*

Someone in authority will tell you, "Nobody has time to read a long message." That might be true. But whether or not people read those long messages, they do respond to them. If you want better fundraising results, a longer message is your best bet.

Fundraising Style Says *You* a Lot—Really, a LOT

In some formal writing styles, it's poor form to address the reader directly. In fundraising, every sentence should be

---

* In dozens of copy-length tests, I've seen the short version do better only once. In email testing, the long version does better a little over half the time, though statistical ties are frequent.

directed to the reader. And many sentences should include the word *you*.

One of the oldest and best self-diagnostics for fundraising copy is to print out your message and do the following:

- ▶ Circle every occurrence of the word *you*.
- ▶ Underline all first-person pronouns (*I*, *me*, *us*, *we*, *our*, and the like).

When you do, you should see lots of circles and few underlines. If you don't, your fundraising copy is out of balance. It's likely to underperform because it fails to address the donor and make the cause about her. (More later on making the donor the focus of the stories you tell.)

Fundraising Style Is Smart about Jargon

Everyone tells you to avoid jargon.

That's good advice, usually. But not always in fundraising.

The right kind of jargon, used in the right way, can make you more believable and persuasive. It can connect you more closely with your donors and help bring in more revenue.

Jargon is nothing other than specialized language. People talk and write in jargon because it's useful.

Those of us who work in direct mail throw around all kinds of jargon, carrier envelope, driver, remit (accent on the first syllable, of course). It's easier that way. We don't have to say, "The envelope that all the other stuff is in when the package mails."

Professions aren't the only groups with jargon. Faith communities and localities have them, too:

▶ Eastern Orthodox Christians talk a lot about "the Theotokos." If you're outside that community, that word is probably Greek to you. If you're inside, it's completely natural.

▶ There's a park in my neighborhood that everyone calls "Big Howe." That's not its official name. Only people who don't live here call it what the Parks Department calls it.

Jargon, like clichés, helps people communicate. It also helps people connect. Using Theotokos or Big Howe with someone else who knows the term shows you're in the same circle. We have something in common. And when you have something in common, you're on your way to better fundraising.

The dark side of jargon shows when it's used in a way that puts your reader outside the circle. That type of jargon is both a barrier to understanding and a signal of exclusion. It doesn't create a fertile ground for compassion and generosity.

Let's look at a term much used in the nonprofit sector: *capacity building*. If you're serious about lifting people out of poverty, you're probably into capacity building.

Nice concept, but it means nothing to your donors. It has no emotional connotations. It only tells them one thing: You're outside my circle.

I doubt most people who use capacity building use it to shut out donors. They simply don't recognize it as jargon. They're deaf to the fact that only specialists like themselves know and use the phrase.

But it hurts anyway.

Here are two things to consider before tossing insider terms into your fundraising:

► Will your audience understand the jargon? It's easy to assume that because you know it, they do too. Not necessarily. Run it past a non-expert to see whether it's understood. You might be surprised.

► Why are you using jargon? Be sure it's not to show donors how smart *you* are, but how smart *they* are.

How Headlines Can Save Human Civilization and Your Fundraising

Headlines are the most important words you write. Advertising legend David Ogilvy put it this way: "On the average, five times as many people read the headline as read the body copy. When you have written your headline, you have spent eighty cents out of your dollar."

Traditional advertising, which relied heavily on newspaper and magazine print ads, developed headline writing into a science. Here's a piece of received wisdom from that era that's still important to know: The headline is the ad for the ad. Nobody will ever read the rest of what you have to say if the headline doesn't pull them in.

They Laughed When I Sat Down
At the Piano
But When I Started to Play!—

A RTHUR had just played "The Rosary." The room rang with applause. I decided that this would be musician himself were speaking to me—speaking through the medium of music—not in words but in chords. Not in sentences but in exquisite melodies! the lessons continued they got easier and easier. Before I knew it I was playing all the pieces I liked best. Nothing stopped me. I could play ballads or classical numbers or jazz, all with equal

This classic headline for a piano correspondence course shows almost every property of a well-written headline.

Print ads are now rare in fundraising, but we all still write a lot of headlines. Not just those in traditional print vehicles like newsletters, but other places that stretch the definition of a headline:

- On Web pages.
- In teaser copy on direct mail envelopes.
- In email subject lines.

Writing good headlines is hard, which is why bad headlines are so common. Here's what I mean:

Partnering with the Southern Philippines

This is a real headline from a nonprofit newsletter. You find headlines like this more often than not. And that's too bad, because it has some real problems:

- There's no news. It's not about a specific event.
- There are no people. Just a region—an abstraction.
- The verb is weak. *Partner* is one of those verbs that conceals action. If you try to visualize what specific action is taking place when someone is partnering, you'll come up blank.
- It's an -ing verb. Even a strong verb loses a lot of its force when you tack -ing onto it. It turns it from an action into a process.

A headline with those problems might as well say this:

Do Not Read This or Your Eyeballs Will Drop Out

Actually, that would be a compelling headline.

Let's turn away from what doesn't work and look at the ingredients of a good headline, starting with what our bad example lacks:

- **News.** Headlines should reveal something of interest, not merely label a situation. It could be news in the journalistic sense (*Last Night's Deep Freeze Sent Crowds of Homeless to Our Shelter*). Or a personal story (*Nick Says His Chemo Is Like Being "Rescued by a Monster"*).
- **People.** Make headlines about people, not situations. Instead of *Drought Strikes Northeast Africa*, make it *Families Flee Worsening Drought*.
- **Strong verbs.** Use one- or two-syllable verbs that show action in a concrete, sensory way. Words like *blast, climb, dance, flee, grab, jolt, limp, mumble, plunge, race, scam-*

*per, tear, wander, yell.** Notice how these words sound like some kind of conflict is going on? That brings us to the next ingredient . . .

- ► **Conflict.** The best headlines (and the stories people want to read) feature conflict.
- ► **Relationships.** The most fascinating thing about people is their relationships. Use headlines to show how people are connected. Relationship words like *Mom, Son, Baby,* or profession words like *Teacher* or *Soldier* make headlines more interesting.
- ► **You.** As often as possible, address your reader.
- ► **Punctuation.** Don't put a period at the end of a headline (it means stop). Go easy on exclamation marks (but don't be afraid to use them). Think twice before asking a question in a headline. If the answer is a simple yes or no, or the question is uninteresting, it falls flat.
- ► **Mystery.** For envelope teasers and email subject lines— places where the reader must take action to get to the rest of the message—it's often best not to tell the news. Instead, create a sense of mystery. One of the most effective envelope teasers I ever wrote was *Letter Enclosed.*

Let's take a look at a handful of powerful headlines from the Web and print worlds. Study them. Imitate them. Learn to think the way their writers think:

---

* While researching the topic of strong verbs, I kept coming across dozens of lists of "strong verbs" that featured words like these: *accomplish, achieve, acquire, activate, adapt* . . . abstract, bureaucratic words. If that's what passes for strong verbs, we're in worse shape than I thought.

Brave Dog Shot Twice Defending the Family She Loves
National Enquirer

Firefighters Smash 2-Day-Old BMW That Was Illegally Blocking Hydrant
Gawker

Murder Suspect Wants Jury to Ignore "Murder" Neck Tattoo
New York Post

Britain's Got Talent Star Was Busted for Smuggling Drugs in Bra to Jailed Gangster Boyfriend
Daily Mirror (UK)

Three Attempts—God Wouldn't Let Me Rob That Bank
New York's Bowery Mission

*   *   *

Crusty, old-school, no-nonsense advertising copywriters spend more time on the ten to twenty words of a headline than they do on the several hundred words of body copy. They understand how important headlines are.

CHAPTER 3

Be SURE about Your Writing

Here's an acronym that'll help you write effective, on-target fundraising materials: SURE. That stands for Simple, Urgent, Repetitive, and Emotional.

Simple

Remember the song about the lady who swallowed a fly—then a spider, then some other creatures until she died from ingesting a horse?

Suppose you worked for a group dedicated to preventing accidents like hers. What would your fundraising message be?

Some would describe the problem as it is in the song:

```
Will you do your part to help prevent the
often fatal tragedy of fly, spider, bird, cat,
dog, goat, cow, and horse swallowing?
```

Getting donors to respond to this message would be an uphill struggle. The complexity of the problem is mind-boggling. The solution isn't obvious.

A better approach would be to talk about the most dramatic part of the problem—the fatal horse:

```
In the next few days, someone—perhaps some-
one you know—will have a serious accident
and end up swallowing a living horse. You
can imagine the trauma and pain as the
horse kicks and thrashes on its way down.
She'll die, of course. . . . Unless you help
rush the emergency care she needs.
```

That's fundraising: asking the donor to help do something she understands.

Some might believe the horse-only description is incomplete. "To give donors the full picture," they'd say, "we should describe all the steps of the tragedy, not just the horse."

That's not fundraising. That's med school. Your donors don't need training to be good donors. They need to know only two things:

1. There's a problem.

2. They can be part of the solution.

If your message obscures that equation with a lot of details, you lose them. That's why simplicity gets the job done.

Urgent

```
One in six Americans struggle with hunger.
```

Maybe you've seen fundraising built on this statement. It's an astounding fact—if you stop and think about it. But that's the problem. You shouldn't have to stop and think to get the full power of a fundraising proposition. Most people won't stop and think.

"One in six" tells us there's a situation. It does so with almost no urgency. It's just a fact. It has all the emotional power of a wad of gum.

The only way to break through the inertia of life is to say something like:

```
Molly is so hungry she can barely focus her
eyes. Her head constantly throbs, and her
stomach feels like an empty, painful hole.
She's exhausted all the time. And it gets
worse every day.
```

This isn't about hunger. It's a picture of someone who's hungry. It's a bad situation that demands response. That's what it takes to move someone from *not giving* to *giving*.

There are two effective ways to inject urgency into your message:

1. Describe the consequences of not acting.

Be vivid and specific about what can happen if the donor doesn't give. If donors can't see the delta between the world without their gifts and the world with the gifts, they have no reason to act.

> If she doesn't get some good food soon, the next stage in Molly's hunger will be worse: Her immune system will weaken. She'll constantly have painful, festering infections. Worse yet, her developing young brain could be irreversibly damaged. Then she'll face the rest of her life impaired, less able to escape the pain.

2. Make the issue time-sensitive.

Show the donor that giving now is better than giving later. Maybe it's a bad situation that will get worse. Or a deadline looming.

> Molly can't wait a few more days to get the nutrition she needs. For a child, going hungry even for a short time can permanently damage her health.

Whatever you do, never throttle back on a sense of urgency. In fundraising, *later means never.* "Think about it" means you don't need to take action.

Repetitive

Did anyone who heard Martin Luther King's "I Have a Dream" speech that August day more than fifty years ago walk away saying, *I wonder what that speech was about?*

Not too many.

The speech rings in our ears to this day because it used one of the best rhetorical tools we have: repetition.

The phrase "I have a dream" is spoken eight times in the seventeen-minute speech. Several other phrases (including "We can never be satisfied" and "Let freedom ring") are also repeated. The result: a memorable, clear, compelling speech that changed America.

Repetition works. Repetition helps ideas take root. Repetition leads people to action.

It's easy to think of our donors as machines. As if our fundraising activates some kind of "on" button. Press it and the donor will comprehend, believe, care, and respond.

That's not how it works. Yes, there's a button, but you have to press it several times to move the donor to action.

If you've ever spent time with an energetic four-year-old, or read *Green Eggs and Ham* to her, you might be thinking, "Repetition is awful! I don't want to inflict it on my donors!"

It's true that repetition can be annoying. But you have to notice it first. Think about how it goes when the four-year-old says, *Can I have ice cream? Can I have ice cream? Can I have ice cream can I have ice cream can I have ice cream?*

It drives you up the wall. But I'm willing to bet that even in that extreme case of repetition, you went through a process:

1. Not hearing.

2. Hearing, but not paying attention.

3. Paying attention.

4. Getting annoyed.

5. Head exploding.

Unless your writing is a lot worse than I bet it is, your fundraising messages will never reach that excruciating level, especially if you use the following outline for fundraising that's repetitive, but not pain inducing:

- ▶ Introduction: why you're writing to the donor.
- ▶ Ask.
- ▶ Description of the problem.
- ▶ Why the donor's gift is needed *now*.
- ▶ Ask.
- ▶ A story that demonstrates the need, using the life of one person as an example.
- ▶ Ask.
- ▶ Word-picture of the change that'll happen when the donor gives.
- ▶ Ask.
- ▶ Reminder that this cause is closely connected with the donor's values.
- ▶ Ask.
- ▶ Conclusion: thank the donor for caring.
- ▶ P.S. Ask again.

That's a lot of asking. And it would be a long message if you included all the elements. But in fact those are the elements of a strong appeal.

There's a chasm between the experience of reading a fundraising message as a professional and reading it as a donor.

You're being paid to pore over every line. But I can guarantee your donor has several things more pressing to do than read every single word you've written. So he skims. Skips whole sentences, paragraphs, and pages. Those six asks in the outline? You're lucky if the typical donor catches a glimpse of one or two of them. If you don't repeat your key points, your donor will likely miss them.

Emotional

When you buy something big, like a car, you might think you put a lot of rational, fact-based thinking into your decision.

That's an illusion. The majority of us use a lot more emotion than rationality when making decisions. Even expensive decisions.

When you shop for a car, you process information with the right side of your brain—the emotional side. You reject one car because it's the same color as Aunt Mildred's terrible pea soup. You're drawn to another because it has a bud vase on the dashboard—classy!

Once you settle on something, the left side of your brain goes to work. It seeks to *justify your emotional decision*. (The car with the bud vase does have low emissions, after all.)

That's how it goes with charitable giving. With *even less* left-brain involvement. After all, giving away your money is an irrational thing to do (if you only look at it rationally).

That's the way donors make their decisions. Don't fight it. Don't try to win them over with facts. When you play that game, you lose every time. You're like a golfer showing up with his clubs at the Super Bowl, hoping to make a touchdown.

Instead, accommodate the way your donors choose. Give them the emotional material they need to make their decision:

- ▶ *Make your message about people, not statistics and facts.* Numbers numb. Stories and pictures of people stir donors to action.
- ▶ *Don't be afraid to tell negative stories.* Your donors give to right wrongs, to turn the tide, to save the day. If your message doesn't break their heart, you're missing the main reason people give: to make a difference.
- ▶ *Editorialize.* Your creative writing teacher insisted, "Show, don't tell." As a fundraiser, you should show *and* tell. Tell them how to feel about it: "This is the saddest situation I've ever seen!" They don't *have to* follow your prompt. But most of them are willing.
- ▶ *Use sensory descriptions.* Write so the reader sees the colors, hears the sounds, smells the odors, and feels the pain of the stories you tell. When you do, you activate mirror neurons, a type of brain cell that gives the sense that someone else's experience is your own. You can help donors know how it feels—even if they've never felt anything like it.

*   *   *

Remember:

Simple.
Urgent.
Repetitive.
Emotional.

I can't claim these four things by themselves will turn
your writing into a fiery-eyed tiger of motivation, but they're
certainly a start.

CHAPTER 4

The Call to Action

I needed a phone. I stood at the counter, credit card in hand. All the sales guy had to do was pull a phone from the shelf and take my money. It would have been his easiest sale of the day.

He wasn't interested in that. "I'm giving you a chance to join some of the most savvy mobile phone users around," he said, a smile frozen onto his face.

"Sure," I pleaded, "but which phone and how much will it cost?"

"All our phones are cutting edge," he answered, apparently speaking to an invisible person next to me who asked better questions. "They're much more than just phones!"

I walked out and gave my money to the phone store next door.

A lot of organizations are exactly that bad at getting our money. They don't offer donors specific reasons to give. Instead, they invite donors to buy into an abstract definition of their cause or to support the organization in a general way.

You've seen fundraising asks like these:

- ▶ Will you help us do our work by sending a generous contribution?
- ▶ Stand with us today in this important cause.
- ▶ Please show your support for our work.
- ▶ Join the movement.

Abstract, non-specific asks are the weakest form of fundraising. And they're common. Little wonder response rates and donor retention are circling the drain for so many organizations.

It used to work. Past generations of donors often gave because giving was their *duty*. It was a civic, religious, or moral obligation. Non-specific asks were good enough. And people trusted institutions.

That's changing. Duty-driven donors are passing. They're being replaced by cynical, strategic, self-oriented "investors" who give to change the world and express their values.

When these individuals give, they expect you to do something specific with their money. They need to be able to picture what it makes possible. And that can't happen unless you put a specific proposition before them.

That's why the fundraising offer—the *call to action* in advertising language—is the foundation of fundraising.

You can muck up almost everything else in your fundraising. You can write boring copy, list rows of statistics instead of telling stories, use clunky design, even violate your brand standards. As long as you have a clear call to action, you'll do okay.

Why Weak Fundraising Works Anyway

Wait a minute, you might be saying. You're telling me a clear call to action is crucial. But I see fundraising *all the time* that doesn't even come close to that. What gives?

It's true. A lot of fundraising has nothing like a specific call to action. And some of it works just fine.

Extraordinary luck? Pact with the devil?

It's because *donors are so charitable* that some are willing to believe in a stirring call to action even when it's *not there*. They supply the emotion, the motivation, and the reasons to act. They do the heavy lifting for you.

When you attend your own child's first recital, it's not a pleasing musical experience. It's excruciating. I speak from experience. Yet those are among the best concerts you'll ever hear. Because you're not listening to the ear-curling reality. You're hearing the potential, filtered through your love. It may sound like a cat choking on a pennywhistle, but you supply the beauty your child can't yet accomplish.

That's what some donors do when they encounter poorly done fundraising. Thank goodness for them. Our organizations would be in deep trouble without these generous souls.

But all is not well: Dropping response and retention rates show us there are fewer of these forgiving donors around today.

But if your message *doesn't* have a fundraising offer, all the creative excellence you can muster hardly matters. You can give a skunk a great haircut and a pedicure, but he's still a skunk.

A strong call to action packages your organization's activities into interesting, attractive, and affordable units. Here are the characteristics of such an offer:

A Fundraising Offer Is Concrete

Think about *shopping*. It's tangible and ultra-specific. Nobody buys *shoes* per se. They buy specific shoes. In specific sizes, styles, and colors. At specific prices. And many people *love* shopping.

Make your fundraising as much as possible like *shopping*, using specificity and concrete details.

Ask the donor to do something she can *see*. Let her provide a needed item. Ask her to take an action. Give her the opportunity to create change. Make progress toward an understandable goal.

Meals for hungry people, not elimination of food insecurity.

If it's possible to take a photo of what you're asking the donor to pay for, you probably have the beginnings of an offer.

An abstraction like "hope" is *not* a fundraising offer. Don't let your call to action be vague like this:

```
Your gift will provide hope for hurting
people.
```

That's like trying to sell a box labeled SHOES, but refusing to provide size, style, or color information. Few shoppers would give it a second's thought. Instead, say something concrete:

```
Your gift will serve piping-hot, nutritious
Thanksgiving dinners—turkey with all the
trimmings—to homeless people down on Skid
Row.
```

The concrete details make it come to life.

A Fundraising Offer Has a Cost

Think of your offer as a specific product. It has specific attributes and a specific cost:

- ▶ $1.79 provides one meal for a hungry person.
- ▶ $14 saves an acre of forest from destruction.
- ▶ $12 sponsors a rescued dog at our shelter.
- ▶ $100 sponsors a viola player at our next concert.
- ▶ $25 moves us closer to the cure.

The cost should be appropriate for each donor's giving level. Don't approach people who are likely to give $25 and ask them to pay $3,000 for a well. Likewise, don't ask a five-figure donor to contribute $25. Either one of these signals to the donor that you don't really know him.

A Fundraising Offer Is a Good Deal

A good deal that increases her impact is one of the best ways to overcome inertia and excite a donor about giving. There are three ways to create a good deal in fundraising:

1. *Cheap.* Whatever you're providing should cost less than it costs in the donor's experience. A meal should be under $2. An entire school might be built for $10,000. It's cheaper for you because you work hard to boost your donors' impact.

2. *Big impact.* Make it clear that every donor's gift—even when small—does a lot of good. It touches a large number of people. Or it touches one person in a big way. It meaningfully changes a situation. *It may only be a meal, but it opens the door to a transformed life.*

3. *Multiplication.* Offers are especially effective when you can tell the donor his dollar will become more than a dollar's worth of good. Offer matching funds or show the donor some way his giving unlocks the contributions of others: one dollar ships $10 worth of donated supplies to where they're needed.

How an Offer Comes to Life

A typical direct mail reply device includes all the ingredients of a fundraising offer. It looks like this:

```
Feed the homeless this Thanksgiving!

Yes! I want to do my part to help our
homeless neighbors this Holiday Season.
Please use my gift to provide hot, nutri-
tious meals. Each meal costs just $1.79, so
enclosed is my gift of

    [ ] $17.90 to provide meals for 10 people
    [ ] $26.85 to provide meals for 15 people
    [ ] $35.80 to provide meals for 20 people
    [ ] $44.75 to provide meals for 25 people
    [ ] Other: $_____
```

Let's look at that reply slip in more detail:

Headline: An attention-grabbing statement that sums up the offer as an attractive action.

Action line: The complete statement of the offer, often written in the donor's voice. The "YES!" at the beginning is more than a tired old cliché—it's a way to help the donor into a positive frame of mind. Most fundraisers write this action line before writing anything else.

Handles: The amounts you're suggesting the donor give, connecting each amount to specific outcomes.

* * *

Here's how important it is to create a great fundraising offer: If your offer is good, you can still succeed even if you're not so sure about everthing else. All that other stuff—from the way you write to your design choices—tends to fall into place behind a strong offer.

CHAPTER 5

The Magic Words

Fundraising has two magic words. One is enchanting, the other has sinister force to weaken your writing. When you control these two words, you can wield wizard-like powers.

The Good Magic Word: You

The power of *you* comes from the fact that good fundraising is always about the *donor*. Your organization's methodology, the competence of your staff, your vision statement, your philosophy, your brand . . . talking about these things isn't really fundraising. At best, these are incidental topics within the conversation about *how the donor is going to change the world.**

Here's a truth about fundraising that some people find distressing: *The reason donors give has more to do with what's going on in their heads than what's going on in your organization.*

---

* The good magic only resides in the singular form of *you*, not the plural, which is lifeless by comparison.

While you struggle to articulate how awesome your programs are, donors' real motivations are like these:

▶ Donor A gives because when he was young, classical music saved him from suicide. Now he's driven to make music as widely available as possible.

▶ Donor B's heart overflows with love for the Virgin Mary. She gives to specific causes because she believes Mary cares especially for young mothers in need.

▶ Donor C is ambivalent about his prosperity. He feels better when he gives to help the poor and disadvantaged.

▶ Donor D gives to prove to herself that she's a better person than her sister.

▶ Donor E survived cancer and gives to celebrate and pay it forward so others may someday overcome the disease.

Don't let the indirect, sometimes illogical nature of these motivations make you think they're inferior. If you do, you'll miss the point of fundraising. Look at your own motivations for giving, and I can almost guarantee you'll find your reasons are similar.

But here's the hard part: We rarely know those inner motivations. Even Big Data doesn't know. You could ask every single donor what's going on in his or her head, and you still wouldn't know. They can't—or won't—articulate it.

That's where the magic of *you* comes in.

When your fundraising is all about how Ms. Donor can change the world through your organization, you dovetail into the story in her head. You may not know Donor A's backstory or Donor D's relationship with her sister, but you're being relevant if you make the message about *them*.

I was once asked to create a fundraising letter template to help novice writers. I struggled for days to come up with a universal outline. Then the solution dawned on me. *Every fundraising message* looks like this:

```
Dear Friend,

You. You. You. You. You. You. You. You. You.
You. You. You. You. You. You. You. You. You.
You. You. You. You. You. You. Yes, you. You.
You. You. You. You. You. You. You. You. You.
You. You. You. You. You. You. You. You. You.

Sincerely,

[Signature]

P.S.      You. You. You. You. You. You. You.
You. You. You. You. You.
```

All you have to do is sprinkle in some interesting nouns, some lively verbs, and a call to action.

Okay, that's not helpful in a practical way, so let me make it a bit more realistic:

```
When you see a homeless person sitting on a
park bench, or sleeping under a bridge, you
wonder what you should do. That's the kind
of person you are.
```

Do you give a homeless person some spare change? Is that kind and helpful, or does it just makes things worse?

That decision is up to you. But let me tell you something you can do that you'll be completely confident is the right thing: <u>Send a gift to cover the cost of having homeless people stay at our shelter</u>.

When you send your gift, you'll know you're meeting real needs, not supporting addictions.

Your donation will make their lives better. Not just for a few minutes, or a day, or even a few weeks. You'll help them find permanent change. Get them off the street and into a joyful, productive new life that every person wants and deserves. You'll improve our whole community.

Even through you tell the donor what your organization does, you make her part of the story.

The Sinister Word: I

That's *I* in all its forms, including *me, we, us, our,* and all the others. This word is the most commonly spoken in English. It can be hard to avoid.

I has evil power in two distinct arenas:

First, if you overuse it, it'll make your message about you or your organization. That's not good fundraising. It reads like this:

```
We are the top provider of services to the
homeless in the tri-county area. Every night
we provide safe, welcoming shelter to more
than 3,000 men, women, and children.
    And our whole-person approach to recov-
ery is the very best way to help the home-
less. Studies show we are 40 percent more
effective at bringing about long-term
change for the homeless than any other pro-
gram in the area.
```

Most of the things that make you great won't move people to action. I'm not saying those things are unimportant. They just don't stir people.

Talking about yourself is poor fundraising, but the evil power of *I* really bubbles from the cauldron when you use it in your office discussions *about* fundraising. When you use *I* statements like these:

- ▶ "I like it."
- ▶ "I don't like it."
- ▶ "I would never respond to that."

How *you* feel about the fundraising *doesn't matter*. Not a whit. What your donors experience is the only thing that matters.

When you base your judgment on your own response, you're sure to get it wrong. You'll make it too complex. Too modern. You'll focus on processes, not outcomes. You'll describe how wonderful things are since your organization got involved. You'll miss the problems your donors can solve.

Almost any time you have the feeling you've said something awesomely persuasive, take that as a sure sign you need to revise.

*   *   *

It can be humbling—almost painfully so—to use the magic words *you* and *I* correctly. It makes your message all about donors, not the cause and organization you're passionate about. It means saying things that motivate them but may not inspire you.

Here's the trick: Learn to get your thrills *not* from fundraising messages that make you or your boss feel good but from the results your work creates. After all, that's your job.

And that's the magic.

CHAPTER 6

The Sound of Writing

I was working on a direct mail appeal about something in Brazil when a phrase popped into my head: "Millions of Brazilians."

I was delighted. I scooted around the office saying "millions of Brazilians" in a goofy, sing-song voice to random coworkers. (You could tell the word people from the non-word people. The former started saying "millions of Brazilians." The others looked at me as though I'd sprouted an elephant trunk.)

Millions of Brazilians is a delightful phrase.* It rhymes. And rhyming phrases are more persuasive and memorable than plain words that have the same meaning.

Haste makes waste? Everyone knows that. Partly because it's true but mostly because it rhymes. Did anybody ever tell you, "When you carelessly rush through your work, you make more mistakes and end up taking longer"? Yes, you've heard

---

* *Millions of Brazilians* has one thing wrong with it: It's about *millions of people*. Big numbers are a mistake in fundraising. More about that later.

that many times. You just don't remember. Good thing you know *haste makes waste.*

If your readers remember what you say and enjoy the way it sounds, your fundraising will do better.

I'm not suggesting you go all Wordsworth and spend hours leafing through a rhyming dictionary. But now and then seek rhyming words and put them near each other.

Like **Give/Live**. That is irresistible for fundraisers looking for rhymes. Corny? Sure. But that doesn't mean it's any less memorable or persuasive.

This online ad from St. Jude Children's Research Hospital features rhyme.

There are other rhymes like that: Sad/Glad, Good/Should, Cancer/Answer.

Make a list of words you're likely to use in your fundraising. Then find rhymes for them. Post your list where you'll see it while you're writing. Sprinkle in the rhymes when it's natural to do so.

Other types of rhyming that can have the same positive effect on your writing:

- ▶ Near rhymes: when the sound match is not exact (Man/Hand)
- ▶ Assonance: matching vowel sounds (Green/Street)
- ▶ Consonance: matching consonants at beginnings of the word (Hungry/Homeless) or at the end (Sing/Long)

Use these sparingly. If they become noticeable they can distract the reader from your message. And when you're writing fundraising, you're a fundraiser before you're a poet.

*   *   *

Letting rhythm flow in your copy can improve its readability and its pleasure factor. Good writing has an easy, forward-moving quality, like a gentle brook rushing over smooth stones.

The best way I know to become good at writing pleasant-sounding, easy-flowing copy is to do two things:

1. *Read a lot.* If you're a writer, I think you're already doing this. Good writing seeps into your consciousness. It'll show in your writing.

2. *Read your copy aloud.* If it sounds clunky or awkward or you find yourself stumbling over words, those are the places to revise for better rhythm.

*   *   *

Nice-sounding copy won't transform weak fundraising, but it might make good fundraising better. By making your messages more pleasing to read, you might encourage a few more fence-sitting donors to drop onto your side of the yard. Perhaps over time, donors will come to think of your organization's messages as easier and more pleasant to read than the usual stuff. And the more they read with a positive attitude, the more likely they are to give.

PART II

Why Stories Matter in Fundraising

Like many people, I spent much of my life believing my father was immortal. Then he told me a story that changed that.

When dad was diagnosed with cancer, I *knew* he was going to beat it. The whole family did. I was worried, of course, and I learned enough about his cancer to realize we couldn't take it lightly. But my heart and most of my mind were confident he'd overcome it. He was in his 60s. I was in my 40s.

For two years it went well. He had a few rounds of chemo that shrank the tumors and kept him in good health. He continued working as a math professor and talked about the future. There were places he wanted to travel, and he looked forward to his grandchildren's milestones. He bought a new car.

Then the cancer roared up like a flame with new fuel. Dad went through an especially aggressive regime of chemotherapy. It left him on his back, gasping and bleeding from his mouth. But it didn't slow the cancer. Still, we believed he would overcome.

My family went to my parents' house for dinner after Dad had recovered from that chemo. It was a completely normal evening. Usual conversation. Dad looked well, almost back to normal. My faith in a positive outcome grew as we ate and talked.

Then after dinner Dad cornered me in the kitchen. Nobody else was around. He grabbed me by both shoulders. That wasn't like him at all. His hands trembled.

"I'm worried about Mom," he said, his eyes drilling into me. "She really can't take care of herself. Last night her sleeve caught fire at the stove. I was there, so she wasn't hurt. But you know how she is. . . ."

He didn't finish the thought. He let it play out in my imagination. We faced each other in silence for probably a minute.

My mother had a chronic illness. All her life she had an impulsive attitude that mostly served her well. But as her abilities faded, her approach was becoming dangerous. Dad had been quietly taking on the increasing burden of her care: driving her to appointments, making sure she took her medications, keeping her from falling, from getting lost, from setting herself afire.

It suddenly hit me—hit me almost with physical force—that my optimistic belief about his cancer was out of step with reality. At that instant, I realized that the cancer might take him, and leave my mother to my care.

That was the moment my father became mortal.

All he'd done was paint a quick verbal sketch: my mother, standing at the stove, flames licking up her sleeve, unaware as it climbed her arm. It was as vivid as a movie.

Until then, I'd understood the risk with my head but hadn't felt it in my gut, or taken it seriously enough to prepare for a future without him. Now I was charged with energy to respond.

That's the power of story. It can flip the switch in our heads from *"It's not quite there"* to *"It's unavoidably **real**."*

My father's story—the last story he ever told me—was barely a story at all. But it was utterly vivid and heavy with urgency. I began to prepare for life without my father. He died a month later, and I became my mother's caregiver.

I hope I never tell a story that hurts a donor as much as that story stung. But I do hope to tell stories that deliver as much motivating truth.

My experience is in no way unusual. We all live parts of our lives hiding behind a curtain. Maybe it's the health of a loved one. Or our own financial situation. Or the appalling fact that children are going hungry. Or that diseases like cancer carry off people far too soon.

We know the facts. We can calculate the statistics. But we know them with our heads, not our hearts. That's how your cause is for most donors. They've been exposed to the facts, probably for decades. You can shovel more and more facts about your issue at them, but you won't change a thing in their brains, their will, or their muscle to pick up a pen and write a check.

Not until you lift the curtain by telling a story. Until then, they won't give.

CHAPTER 7

The Elements of a Well-Built Story

For more than two thousand years, writers have been studying Aristotle's *Poetics*. It's a small book that defines the ingredients of powerful stage drama. The ideas in *Poetics* apply to any serious story aimed at touching the heart of an audience.

Call me crazy, but I'm going to reinterpret *Poetics* here because, with some differences, fundraising stores are just like other stories. If Aristotle had worked in our field, I'm sure he would have recognized this.

A fundraising story is made of these main ingredients:

One Protagonist—Aristotle's character or *ethos*
A good fundraising story is about one person.* It's not a village, a neighborhood, or a drought-stricken region. Not the Arts or Democracy. It must be one person we can look in the eye and feel empathy toward.

---

* That "person" can be an animal.

Aristotle wrote the book on telling certain kinds of stories so they are memorable, emotionally resonant, and life changing.

If your story is about the big picture, you short-circuit your donors' ability to feel connected. The human brain can only take in one person at a time:

- One hungry child, not World Hunger.
- One polar bear that can't find a patch of ice, not Climate Change.
- One homeless person who needs a place to stay, not Homelessness.
- One person fighting to overcome cancer, not Cancer.

This one-person rule is nearly ironclad. If you stretch your one person to two—say, you have a wonderful story about a young girl in need and you make her baby brother the costar—you weaken the story and the response.

While fundraising stories should *focus* on one person, most have other people in them: family members, teachers, doctors, and whatever bad guys interact with the protagonist. That's okay. Just make sure the protagonist stays center stage. Make the other people less visible:

- ▶ If someone's role in the story isn't crucial to the story, leave that person out.
- ▶ Don't describe how secondary people look (unless their appearance is part of the story).
- ▶ Don't use secondary people's names (unless it's necessary to avoid confusion).

By un-focusing secondary people in the story, you sharpen the focus on the protagonist.

Let's say your protagonist is a young girl in a poverty-burdened Third World village. Her name is Sumita. She spends almost her entire day doing physical labor at the family home and farm—mostly carrying water from a community well five miles away. She has a mother, a father, four siblings. There's a teacher in the village who knows her and believes in her potential and is encouraging her to go to school.

In your story, we should only meet Sumita and possibly the teacher (who is best called "the teacher" rather than given a name). Leave out her parents, siblings, and others unless they say or do something that's part of the story.

The Curse of the "Bad Mom"

There's one kind of story sure to hurt your fundraising: a "Bad Mom" story. The one about a mother who abandoned, neglected, or abused her children.

In my experience, a story about a bad mom depresses response every time. Here's how varied and terrible my experiences have been with bad mom stories:

- It doesn't work even if the mom in the story has changed her ways and is now an inspiring person in every way.
- It doesn't work even if the bad mom's behavior is the result of forces outside her control.
- It doesn't work even if you focus on the children— the innocent victims.

Nothing makes a bad mom story work. My theory: A bad mom is just *too much*. At some basic, preternatural level, she departs too far from the way things ought to be. Bad mom generates anti-sympathy. And that undermines compassion.

Oddly enough, you can tell stories about bad dads. Or bad women, as long as they aren't mothers. You can tell your donors about reformed murderers, war criminals, liars, thieves, polluters, just about any kind of person—just as long as they aren't bad moms. It's not right, logical, or fair. But it's the reality.

Avoid bad mom stories.

A Problem—Aristotle's plot or *mythos*

Until we see the protagonist struggling with a problem, you still don't have a story.

Just as it's important to focus on one protagonist, you must focus on one concrete problem. Not something global like *injustice* or *poverty*. Not even a narrower issue like *gender inequality*. Those are abstractions.

That means you show the immediate problem as it plays out in the life of your protagonist.

Let's say Sumita is illiterate and uneducated. As long as she stays that way, her only contribution to the family is her physical labor. But it's not too late for her to learn, and she dreams of going to school. Her family is reluctant. They're afraid of losing her labor. They believe education isn't appropriate for a girl.

This is a classic account of gender inequality perpetuating poverty. But that's not how it should feel to your readers. They should experience a straightforward story about the suffering of one girl named Sumita.

The other crucial thing about the problem in your story is you must show it to be *solvable*. By the donor.

Think about that and how it applies to your cause. Have you been appealing to donors to do something they know they can't do? Or have you been presenting them with problems they can solve?

Your donors likely feel powerless to put an end to poverty or injustice. But they can easily imagine reaching out to one person and making a difference.

Details—Aristotle's spectacle or *opsis*

Details make stories real, believable, and memorable.

When you reveal details that engage the senses, you draw the donor deeper into the story. The reader can feel Sumita's pain as if it's her own.

In Sumita's story, some of the details might be:

▸ The unbearable heat and the sweat trickling down her back.

▸ The flies that cluster on every bit of her exposed skin while she crouches next to the water hole.

▸ The weight of the water she carries and how it's deforming her spine, bending her back into a permanent S-shape.

▸ The clean, uniformed children Sumita sees and hears as she trudges past the school.

These details can bring life to a story that otherwise might not be memorable.

Commentary—Aristotle's melody or *melos*

In the dramas of Aristotle's day, there was always a chorus that would interrupt to sing or chant about what was going on. Their job was to make sure the audience didn't miss or misinterpret the point.

As the storyteller engaged in fundraising, *you are the chorus*. It's up to you to help your donor interpret the story. There are two main ways to do that:

▸ *Background information* that gives context. In Sumita's story, she can't go to school like your kids do. The fees for uniforms, books, and supplies are beyond the reach of her family. Chances are your reader doesn't know this. When you tell her, the story becomes stronger.

▶ *Emotional content.* Tell the reader how to feel. You can do this with simple asides like, *How would you feel if you were Sumita?* Or, *My heart breaks for Sumita!*

The Right Ending—Aristotle doesn't include this one on his list

Your fundraising story should *not* end with the problem solved. It should end unresolved, a cliffhanger, waiting for the donor to take action. Many fundraising stories, otherwise well told, fall down on this point.

If you show the problem has been taken care of, you resolve the tension you worked so hard to build. You're saying clearly, *Never mind.*

This is a challenge because by the time you discover the story, the hard part of it is usually past. Most likely, you learned about Sumita because she's in school now, where someone interviewed her. Of course there's another girl who's still waiting. But we haven't met her yet!

Fundraisers often try to solve this problem in this way:

```
Sumita finally got into school. She's doing
well, excelling in math. But thousands more
like her still need help.
```

Logically, that solves the problem. Emotionally, it doesn't. The story of Sumita getting her problem solved is still the story. It's more vivid than your weak disclaimer about faceless thousands. In essence, you shouted that everything is fine, then vaguely mumbled that maybe it isn't. What does the donor hear? You guessed it.

You can't slap an untrue ending on the story, claiming that Sumita is still waiting for help if she isn't. Instead, you have to do something very hard to do: *Not tell the end of the story.* Just leave it untold.

I realize this violates your instincts as a writer. It leaves unanswered a question readers will ask. That can make them, and you, uncomfortable.

But it's smart fundraising. And by leaving the ending off, you're letting the reader enter the story and choose the happy ending he wants.

Let's look at the ending of Sumita's story as it might appear in a fundraising message:

```
Sumita sat in the shade of a big tree just
outside the school. She could hear the
children inside chanting their arithmetic
lesson. She couldn't understand what their
words meant. A tear ran down her cheek. "I
will never be able to go to school," she
thought, staring at her heavy water can.

  Your gift will send children to school.
You can wipe away those tears and replace
them with happy dreams about the better
life they're building—because of you.
```

*   *   *

Aristotle also believed in a deeper purpose for telling stories. He called it *catharsis*—a sort of psychological cleansing that leads to transformation. He said the intense emotions and situations in a well-told story could change the listeners' lives. In theory, you were supposed to leave an ancient Greek drama weeping and vowing to become a better person.

As fundraisers, we're not quite that ambitious. But almost. We know charitable giving can transform donors' lives, which is why our stories matter so much.

CHAPTER 8

Five Ways to Use Stories for Impact

Have you ever wondered why *Hamlet*, a huge story full of action and violence, starts with a slew of minor characters running around like idiots, thinking they've seen a ghost?

Not to second-guess Shakespeare, but it's because great stories aren't just characters and action. Structure also plays a role—the way they're put together, how you lead in and lead out.

It's the same with fundraising stories. You can get more out of them—more impact, more connection with donors, more donations—by the way you use stories in your messages.

Here are five ways that can maximize their persuasive power:

In Media Res

That's Latin for "in the middle of things," and it describes the way stories often unfold in novels and movies. They don't waste time setting up the context. Instead, they throw you into the exploding helicopter and let you discover who's who and what's what as the story moves along. In a fundraising message, it might go something like this:

```
Dear Friend,

Sweat trickled down Marika's forehead and
stung her eyes. She tried to blink it away,
and that's when he appeared between two
trees—a magnificent mountain gorilla, a sil-
verback, gliding slowly across the clearing.
His black eyes fixed on hers.
```

This is a popular way to write stories in fundraising. Writers choose it because it mimics the literary stories they admire.

I *don't* recommend this approach. I've seen too many well-written fundraising messages start this way and fail. There are three reasons it doesn't work:

1. It's not natural. People almost never tell stories without some sort of introduction or permission. If a stranger walks up and launches into an anecdote, you question his mental stability. Most stories should start with something like, "The most incredible thing happened on my way to work this morning."

2. The story has to be a real blockbuster to pique readers' interest and keep them enthralled without knowing its

purpose. Few stories have the horsepower to carry that off.

3. The story doesn't answer the question donors need answered before they're willing to spend any more time with you: *"Why are you writing to me?"* When you let that question hang there, donors drop away, like sand through an hourglass.

I won't say *never* start a message this way. It can work if the story so completely captures donors' attention that they willingly float along on the current. But that's rare. There are more effective ways to position your story.

In Media Res Interruptus

This is a slight twist on the approach above, one that's almost always more effective.

Start in the middle of things but *quickly* step out of the narrative and address the donor directly. This allows you to create context and answer the *why are you writing to me* question. It might begin this way:

```
Dear Friend,
    Sweat trickled down Marika's forehead
and stung her eyes. She tried to blink it
away, and that's when he appeared between
two trees—a magnificent mountain gorilla, a
silverback, gliding slowly across the clear-
ing. His soulful black eyes fixed on hers.
```

```
I'll tell you what happened next in a
moment, but first I have some very good news
about the part you can play in keeping this
beautiful animal alive and free as it ought
to be.
```

I've seen this approach work many times. When you have a strong story, this structure helps you take advantage of the drama while approaching readers in a way that'll encourage them to stay with you.

Tease and Return

An even more reader-centric way to structure your message and story is to first address the reader directly, give the reason you're writing, and then tell the story.

```
Dear Friend,

You are going to love what I have to tell
you today about how you can help save rare
mountain gorillas from extinction.

But before that, I have some good news about
the part you can play in keeping this beau-
tiful animal alive and free as it should be
be. Like the one our head researcher encoun-
tered recently. . . .
```

```
Sweat trickled down Marika's forehead and
stung her eyes. She tried to blink it away,
and that's when he appeared between two
trees—a magnificent mountain gorilla, a sil-
verback, gliding slowly across the clearing.
His soulful black eyes fixed on hers.
```

This is a natural way to tell a story. It mixes the telling with real life. You seek permission and then launch into the story once you've established a connection with the reader. It's a slower start, but remember you're writing to request funds—not to entertain.

Shuffled Story

Here's another approach where you alternate between telling the story and speaking directly to the reader. In this case, you go back and forth between the two modes. It might go like this:

```
Dear Friend,

Sweat trickled down Marika's forehead and
stung her eyes. She tried to blink it away,
and that's when he appeared between two
trees—a magnificent mountain gorilla.

As a friend of the Society, you stand right
next to her every day in the work of saving
endangered apes.
```

You would have been just as thrilled as she was when she saw him: a silverback, gliding slowly across the clearing, his soulful black eyes fixed on hers.

You'll also be glad to know that your donation will keep her and our other researchers at work in the field, keeping this beautiful animal alive and free as it ought to be.

This approach has a distinct challenge: to maintain momentum with the story even though you keep breaking away from it (this, however, is why you earn the big bucks).

After Everything Else

This is the simplest way to use a story. Don't let that deter you from doing it. Simple is good.

Cover everything else you need to cover and then tell the story. Here's an outline:

- ▶ Why I'm writing.
- ▶ Why the situation is urgent.
- ▶ Ask.
- ▶ Why you'll be glad you gave.
- ▶ Story.
- ▶ Ask again.

This pushes the story to the middle (or even the end) of the message. That's okay. Telling the story after you've covered everything else (or nearly everything) should be the default way to handle stories in fundraising.

*   *   *

The best fundraising writers respect stories, but they don't fall in love with them. And they never treat stories like they're some kind of sorcery that automatically makes anything work. Even the best story is just one of several tools you use to build a powerful fundraising appeal.

CHAPTER 9

How Storytellers Tell Stories

Uncle Herb, the family storyteller, kept three generations spellbound at the dinner table. We'd sit and listen long after the kitchen chairs became noticeably hard and uncomfortable.

You'd come away from an Uncle Herb story session thinking, "He's had such an *interesting* life." But in reality his life was ordinary. He was a decent man who raised a good family in the American Midwest. He served in the Army but never saw action or left the country. He had a long career as a machinist at a series of midsized factories you've never heard of.

Most of his stories were ordinary events that had happened recently—"Just last Thursday" or "The week after Christmas." They were anecdotes about his encounters with friends and coworkers—funny, strange, or telling exhibits of human nature. The kinds of things that happen to all of us, but most of us don't polish them into stories.

Uncle Herb's secret wasn't a rich, picaresque technique. With his meandering narratives, Uncle Herb was a straight-line descendent of cave-dwelling storytellers—those who kept the clan entertained around their fitful campfire while saber-toothed tigers prowled the darkness outside.

If you're willing to borrow some of Uncle Herb's time-honored techniques, you can tell powerhouse colloquial stories that grab donors' attention and prepare them to take action.

He Pulled the Listener into the Narrative

Uncle Herb punctuated his stories with asides directed at specific listeners. He'd lean over, rest his heavy hand on your shoulder and say, "You'll love what the cop said to me next." And sure enough, it would be something that especially tickled you.

Uncle Herb understood that every listener to every story tells his own inner narrative. She evaluates the story she's hearing. She considers its meaning and significance and explores how it supports (or affronts) her values and beliefs. When Uncle Herb knew you, he'd find something in his story that he hoped would click with you, and he'd point it out.

Addressing the listener (reader) this way enriches his or her experience of the story. It grows more relevant and meaningful, because it connects with the listener's inner narrative. It also guides the listener's interpretation of the story. You're saying, *This is why the story I'm telling matters to you.*

You aren't Uncle Herb, facing a small circle of relatives or friends you know personally. But most donor audiences share values and beliefs. You can make decent guesses about what in your story draws them in and makes them part of it:

```
Not everyone can look into the eyes of a
great ape and appreciate the mind that's
so nearly like yours and mine. But you can.
That's why I believe you're one of those rare
people who understands the importance of
helping the apes.
```

He Was in His Stories, but Not Too Much

All of Uncle Herb's stories were told in the first person. But he was never the star. He was usually an observer, a foil, or a straight man. Because he was in the story, he was able to add color.

Flowery language wasn't in his toolbox, so he made his descriptions rich with firsthand observations. Instead of just telling us it was cold, he would say, "My fingers got so cold I couldn't bend them!"

He inserted these comments judiciously, so he didn't turn the story into a monologue about himself. That wouldn't have been as interesting.

Here's how you might do the same in a fundraising story:

```
I've been in that same forest preserve and
listened to the calls of the gorillas echo-
ing through the mountain mists. Let me tell
you, it gives me goose bumps just to think
```

```
about it now. Those amazing animals really
do have a connection with you and me.
```

Telling stories in the first person, rather than the third person, is a good choice in fundraising.

The Structure of His Stories Was Clear

You always knew where you were while Uncle Herb's stories unfolded. He made sure of that, often by telling you what the climax was going to be: "Let me tell you about the guy at the hardware store who poured an entire gallon of pink paint over his head." Knowing the climax of the story, you could watch it unfold.

If you've ever squirmed through a speech or sermon where you had no idea whether it was going to last another five minutes or thirty, you know how important a clear structure is for the listener. Don't do that with your fundraising stories. Give your readers signposts of the structure:

```
When the great silverback hunkered down in
the brush a few feet away from Marika, she
thought it was the most exciting moment of
her life. It was about to get a lot more
exciting.
```

His Stories Ended on Time

Even Uncle Herb's most complex and involved stories didn't seem long. You never started wondering, How much longer will this last?

He kept them short but complete.

How long should a fundraising story be? I can only answer with the answer Abraham Lincoln is said to have given when asked "How long are your legs?" Honest Abe said, "Long enough to reach the ground."

His Stories Were True

Uncle Herb's brother Hubert was also a storyteller. In some ways he was even better than Herb. But eventually everyone discovered Uncle Hubert's fatal flaw: His stories were made up.

There's nothing wrong with fiction. Sometimes it rings truer than truth. But when you hear an amazing tale that seems to be true, and then discover it's fiction, you feel *taken*. It's a lie.

The lack of reality was what gave Hubert the early advantage over Herb. His stories were more exciting and more tightly structured. But eventually everyone would sniff out they weren't true. They regarded his stories as not worth listening to, despite his craftsmanship.

Fundraising stories have to be true. If they aren't, you're toying with people's emotions. That's uncool as well as unethical. And your falsity will be sniffed out just as surely as Uncle Hubert's always was.

CHAPTER 10

The Hero of the Story

There's a decision every writer makes before starting a story. If you make the right choice, your story can be a cupid's arrow aimed at the donor's heart. Make the wrong choice and you'll spoil any magic, leaving the story as exciting as a sponge soaked with cold coffee.

That decision: *Who is the hero of the story?*

I don't mean a character with a cape and a weird backstory. I mean the protagonist, the person you want the reader to care about. The hero may be strong or weak. He may triumph, or (somewhat more likely in fundraising) she may experience defeat, pain, or loss. But in every case, the hero is the star of your appeal.

I'll focus here on three hero types that most often show up in fundraising stories. Then we'll examine how each type transforms its story—for good or for ill.

Organization as Hero

Most fundraising stories make the organization the hero. It's a way to showcase the effectiveness of the group. It goes something like this:

> When I met Robina, I made her a promise. <u>We will take care of your children after you're gone.</u>
>
> It wasn't an empty promise. We were already at work in her village in Uganda when the HIV/AIDS pandemic started killing everyone between the ages of 17 and 60.
>
> Tragically, Robina died two weeks later. But I'm glad to say we're working with her five children through our thriving programs for the hundreds of HIV/AIDS orphans in the village. We're helping them build sustainable, hope-filled futures through:
>
> - Income generation
> - Economic development
> - Civil society training
>
> And that's just the beginning. . . .

There's not much good I can say about this story. It's cold and flat and lacks drama. But that's how stories often go when you make your organization the hero.

Of course, the writer might disagree. She made the organization the hero of the story for a reason. She believes that if she makes it clear how great her organization is, donors will understand and be moved to give.

Sounds reasonable. But it's a big mistake. The underlying assumption is wrong.

Donors don't give because you're excellent. They give because *they* are excellent, and *you help them realize their awesome selves.**

Let me repeat that point, because it's one of the most important, yet least understood, truths about fundraising. *Donors don't give to you because you're excellent. They give because they are.* Your work aids their excellence—you're a channel through which they change the world.

Fundraising writers who understand that truth and build their copy around it usually succeed.

When you tell an organization-as-hero story, what you say is mostly irrelevant to donors. At best it's boring. Sometimes it's even annoying.

But there's more downside. When you make the organization the hero of your story, something happens to the quality of your writing:

▶ The pronouns get out of whack: The word *you* disappears and the unpleasant royal *we* creeps in like a smelly fungus.

▶ Professional jargon (like *pandemic*, *sustainable*, and *civil society*) sprouts all over the place. That's the language of your staff, but not donors.

---

* Make no mistake—you'd better *be* excellent to deserve their support and fulfill their intention.

▶ Human drama takes a backseat to program details. Actually, human drama usually gets kicked out of the vehicle entirely.

▶ There are almost always bullet points used to organize complex information about processes. After all, your processes are hallmarks of your excellence.*

The temptation to make your organization the hero is strong. Your colleagues work hard and are true experts. Some of them, possibly including your boss and board members, want your fundraising copy to reflect the world as they understand it. They honestly believe if you can just capture the excellence of the organization, everyone in the world will gladly donate.

If that weren't enough to throw you off course, you may have brand guidelines that enforce organization-as-hero as the only allowable platform. This is an increasingly common problem among nonprofit organizations.

*   *   *

Beneficiary as Hero

Another common hero in fundraising is a beneficiary. That's someone who is helped or served by the organization—which means, by extension, he or she is helped by the donor. Here's an example:

---

* Don't get me wrong about bullet points—they're a great way to make your writing easy to read. But sometimes they're a crutch you grab when your copy is not about people.

When Robina's husband began to lose weight, she knew he had AIDS. And that meant two things: That he had a few weeks to live, and she had only a little more time than he did. She died about a month after I met her.

A mother of five young children, Robina lived on an island in Lake Victoria, in Uganda. AIDS had swept through the village like a fire, leaving almost no one alive between the ages of 17 and 60.

Robina nodded politely when I visited her dirt-floor, one-room hut. Hollow-eyed, skeletal, she sat motionless on a mat in the dark. Only her eyes seemed alive—and they were full of sadness.

Her greatest fear, she told me, wasn't her coming death, but what was ahead for her children. Her frail, elderly mother had agreed to care for them. But how could she possibly provide for so many?

Most people would agree this story is stronger than the organization-as-hero story. More emotionally resonant and interesting.

But do we hear angels singing the victory hymn? Not quite. There's a fundamental problem with most beneficiary-as-hero stories.

They often become a *writer-as-hero* story, showcasing his or her command of language.

Here's a disturbing truth you should know. Hardly anybody cares how well you write. A few English teachers maybe and an occasional colleague. That's about it. The rest of the world doesn't even notice.

Polished, workshop-style writing that's vivid and dramatic *isn't the way normal people write.* It's even further from the way people *talk.* Write in this way and you build a wall between your cause and your donor.

When you use the refined techniques of fiction, your writing can come across as fiction. Not in the sense that readers think it's untrue, but the tone gives it the flavor of entertainment. Less real.

Think of it this way: If the FedEx guy left a note on your door written in Homeric couplets, you'd pay less attention to when he was coming back with your package and more wondering what the heck was up with him. His style would interfere with his communication.

Writing style aside, the beneficiary-as-hero story is *just another story.* It's one of dozens of stories your reader will encounter on any given day—true stories in the news, anecdotes told by friends, even fiction from television or books. To tell a story is to enter a crowded, noisy space.

If yours is the most jaw-dropping story among several hundred stories it's competing with, then it has a chance to break through all the noise.

Good luck with that.

Fortunately there's a hero who matters much more to your donor, and that turns your story into motivational gold.

*   *   *

Donor as Hero

If the organization makes a poor hero and a beneficiary is only slightly better, what's left? *The donor.* This is the hero the fundraising wizards choose every time. A donor-as-hero story goes like this:

> I wish you could have met Robina. You would have understood her completely, even though her life was very different from yours.
>
> I say "was" because Robina died a month after I met her. Like so many people in her village in Uganda, she died of AIDS. Only elderly people and children were left alive after the disease swept through.
>
> While Robina sat in her dirt-floor hut dying, she had one terrible worry: What about the children? Who will care for my five little ones?
>
> Her elderly mother, of course, would do her best. But how could she care for so many?
>
> That's why I'm coming to you.

Notice that this story is about a beneficiary. But see how the point of view has shifted? The reader has become part of the story. The narrative is happening in *the donor's world*. Address the donor directly and put the story in her context. The details you choose to show are things you'd tell a friend or your mother, not necessarily what you'd include for their symbolic or dramatic value.

In almost every way, the writing is radically unlike either organization-as-hero or beneficiary-as-hero copy:

▶ It's colloquial. Not self-consciously written the way a beneficiary-as-hero story often is.

▶ There's a lot of *you* in it, because without the donor the story is empty.

▶ It directly answers the question "Why are you telling me this?"

▶ It easily and gracefully integrates with a call to action. It's *all about action*—not what the organization is doing, but what the donor can do.

When you make the donor the hero of your story, these good things happen to the copy almost automatically. It's the writing equivalent of starting your day with a good breakfast.

*   *   *

Here's the secret behind all fundraising storytelling: Don't brag about the awesomeness of your organization and don't demonstrate your mad skills as a writer. Instead, connect with the donor and invite him into a corner of the world that he can change.

CHAPTER 11

Word Pictures

B e honest. While you're reading about the wonders that stories can do for fundraising, you may be saying, *That's fine in theory, but my organization doesn't have the resources to gather these great stories.* Or maybe even *Get real, Brooks! We don't get stories like you're describing—ever!*

Okay, you're right. That's the situation for most fundraising writers.

Worse yet, in some organizations, access to stories is granted only to "important" people rather than the writer who actually does something with them. Or someone has mandated against the kind of stories that motivate giving because they violate the brand or make insiders uncomfortable.

There's no easy solution if you face these barriers. You need to navigate culture, attitudes, and personalities, usually with charm and tact. But there is a workaround, and it's pretty good: word pictures.

Word pictures are the mac and cheese of fundraising copy. It's not the tastiest cuisine, but in a pinch it can do the job.

A word picture is *almost* a story. It's not a specific account of a specific person. It lacks the documentation of a journalistic account or the richness of a narrative. It's just a snapshot. A few sentences that reveal a situation and capture its human and emotional core.

To gather the raw material for a story, someone has to witness it. Remember the tale of Robina in the last chapter? We learned she had five children. She lived in a dirt-floor, one-room hut. Her eyes were full of sadness.

Someone had to walk into her hut, talk to her, hold her hand, and look her in the eyes to discover these details.

Suppose we'd never been to Uganda and never met Robina. Instead, we had a situation report about her community and how AIDS had been raging through the area. It would tell us facts about the economy and demographics of the area. It would report that virtually everyone who wasn't a child or elderly was dead or dying of AIDS. That there was a swelling population of orphans without sufficient care.

Those facts don't add up to a story. But you could use them to create a word picture:

```
Let me tell you how it is: A young mother
sits wearily in her small house near Lake
Victoria in Uganda. She has AIDS. She knows
she has only a few weeks left to live. She
worries about her children—who will care
for them when she's gone?
```

That isn't as rich as the story you read earlier about Robina. But it may be *good enough* to touch a donor's heart and stir her to action.

The characteristics of a word picture that are different from a full-grown story are these:

- ► The way you set up a word picture is different. You must make it clear that this isn't a specific account. Use introductory phrases like "Imagine," "Picture this," "If you were there, you'd see."
- ► No plot. It's a photo, not a movie. You're just capturing the situation.
- ► It's told in present tense. That helps to signal the ongoing nature of the scene. Past tense signals that you're describing a specific event that happened in the past.
- ► It's short. Seldom more than five or six sentences.
- ► It's missing names. When you give someone a name, you signal that this is a specific person.

The tricky and complicated thing about word pictures is that it's easy to cross the line into making stuff up. We can't do that. It's unethical and breaks the relational contract we want to build with donors (remember Uncle Hubert). Even *seeming* to make stuff up can hurt those relationships.

That's why I want to take a close look at what separates this word picture from a real story. The word picture used these details:

- ► *A young mother.* From the facts in the situation report, we know that the problem involves a lot of parents. So when we show a young mother, we're showing someone we know is really there.

- ▶ *Sits wearily.* Fatigue is a symptom of HIV/AIDS, so we can confidently say that someone suffering from late-stage AIDS would be weary.
- ▶ *In her small house.* The economic condition of the community makes it clear that just about every home is small. Characterizing the home as a hut, as we did in the story, might be okay if we had knowledge that everyone in the community lives in a hut.
- ▶ *A few weeks to live.* AIDS progressed quickly in that time and place. Anyone diagnosed with it had a life expectancy counted in weeks.
- ▶ *Worries about her children.* Any mother in that situation would worry. That's a safe assumption to make. You might argue that a worried mother would have a worried expression, as Robina did. I can't make that leap because in this case, we never saw that detail.

This may seem to be a hair-splitting exercise, but it's important to make word pictures as vivid as possible and to be able to support your claims.

There's a kind of smell test that can help us divine the difference between a reasonable supposition and making stuff up: when you read a word picture, ask: *How do I know this?*

Is each detail and the overall impression reasonable and widespread? Or are you inadvertently creating a sense of specificity that's not real?

A well-built word picture can give your readers an emotional connection nearly as powerful as a real story. It has all the active ingredients: people, a problem, and emotion. That gets you most of the way to where you need to go.

Granted, a good story is better than a word picture any day. More powerful, more persuasive, more relevant. But a vivid word picture is better than a dull, confusing, or off-point story. And a word picture is far better than no story at all.

PART III

What We're Really Doing: The Psychology of Fundraising

For four days I'd been scrambling up muddy paths to threadbare houses and broken mobile homes in rural Kentucky. At each place, I interviewed people mired in poverty.

I was collecting stories for a social-service agency in Appalachia. I knew I'd see deep poverty and broken lives. But I wasn't feeling sympathy or connection. The sameness of people's stories was getting to me. They'd all been dealt bad hands in life, but their responses were so self-destructive. Many of them bubbled with hatred for minorities, liberals, and the government. *If I hear one more racist rant*, I thought, *I'm not sure I can finish this job.*

As we approached a peeling house, dogs boiled out from under the porch, yelling like soldiers on the attack. They surrounded me, growling, teeth bared. A nine-year-old boy with a shaved head crawled from under the porch. "What you want," he said in a monotone.

My guide, a social worker who knew the family, explained that we were there to visit his grandfather. The boy called off the dogs and walked away.

In the house, the floor sagged, sinking like a mattress beneath each step. A Confederate flag covered the main window, staining everything red. A television blared a witless game show. It was unbearably stuffy.

The grandfather, sunk deep in a peeling vinyl recliner, had terminal cancer—I never learned what type. A few questions into the interview, with no prompting at all, he started to blame his disease on ethnic minorities and socialists. I pretended to take notes while he wheezed on.

Finally exhausted, he lit a cigarette and started smoking through a hole in his throat. He had to pinch the wound around the cigarette to inhale. Each drag ended in a fit of coughing, smoke flushing from his nose, mouth, and the hole in his throat.

I turned away. How could I make donors care about this hate-filled man? My own empathy had run dry. The way these people seemed to despise everyone, including themselves, I just couldn't find a compassionate hook in any of them. I felt I'd hit the low point of my career.

Then something caught my eye. The social worker took the man's hand and squeezed it. An ordinary gesture. She smiled at him; he looked up and smiled back. I got a sensation like you get from those "magic eye" pictures, when the visual noise suddenly resolves into an image—it was there all along.

The person in the chair suddenly stopped being a bitter, self-destructive caricature. He turned into a man. Which, of course, he'd been the whole time.

It wasn't much. I might have missed it if I'd been looking away. But that small gesture put it back together for me. It didn't matter what I thought of him—he was a human in need, and I was a writer about need. I could tell his story the way it deserved to be told—pushing aside my own misgivings and prejudices. I could help donors see him, too, without leading them into the forest I'd been wandering.

That's our job as fundraising writers. We start with complex, confusing, even discouraging realities and then transform them into living opportunities for donors. We build bridges that connect people to causes they care about. Bridges that allow understanding, love, and money to cross the gap.

That's hard to do, because we writers labor under the same limitation as everyone else—the human impulse to make everything about ourselves.

What does a West Coast, espresso-sipping professional writer have to do with a gun-toting mountain man dying of cancer? Not much. Because he's so far removed from me, so different from me, his mind full of thoughts strange to me, it's easy to disparage him or ignore him. Until I find a way to see him and care. The best fundraising writers figure out how to cross those canyons.

The next few chapters will focus on ways we can approach donors and giving. We'll take a look at what's going on under the surface, in the subconscious, paying special attention to:

▶ "Fundcrushing," the evil twin of fundraising that can keep you from connecting with donors.

▶ A balanced approach to fundraising that avoids the extremes of over-negative and over-positive messages.

▶ How to harness guilt in fundraising. (Spoiler alert: You pretty much can't.)

▶ A number of assumptions you should make about donors if you want to truly connect with them.

We've been dwelling on the way good fundraising writing looks, sounds, and feels. Now let's dig below the surface and see how good fundraising writing *works*.

CHAPTER 12

The Evil Cousin of Fundraising

How often have you read fundraising built on statements like these?

- ► 31,000 children die from hunger every day.
- ► There are 9,500 homeless people in our community.
- ► 11,000 Americans die of cancer every week.
- ► 2.7 million healthy cats and dogs are euthanized in the U.S. every year.

These are meant to stir you to action by bowling you over with big numbers. The organizations seem to think, *People will open their wallets once they know how big the problem is!*

It doesn't work.

In fact, big-number fundraising is so bad it shouldn't be called "fundraising." *Fundcrushing* is more like it. It's a force for evil, training people that charitable giving is for dummies. Fundcrushing spreads a message of apathy and hopelessness.

Let's look at some of the differences between the two approaches:

Fundraising	Fundcrushing
You can change the world. Here's how.	The problem is *huge* beyond imagining. Just look at those overwhelming numbers!
Meet this person you can help.	Grasp the enormity of the problem.
Give because you can be part of the solution.	Give because this problem is so big.
Feel empowered.	Feel unimportant and guilty.

Fundcrushing discourages people from giving becase it ignores two facts about human motivation:

1. *Facts* don't move people to give. We give when we respond emotionally to a situation. Facts suppress emotions.

2. People don't rise to action because a problem is *big*. They take action because they see a problem as *solvable*. Telling them the problem is big in effect tells them it's *not solvable*.

The Exception

There's an exception to the rule that numbers demotivate: large-scale natural disasters. Earthquakes that level cities and kill tens of thousands. Hurricanes that rake the coast and wash away homes and people.

In these cases, the fundraising *is* all about numbers. Especially the number of people killed.

There's a reason for this ghoulish state of affairs. Large casualty counts drive more media coverage. More media coverage means more awareness. And more awareness means more people give.

During a disaster and its aftermath, the news media do a large part of our job for us. They confront everyone with the disaster and its human suffering. Everywhere you look, you see haunting photos of disaster victims and hear wrenching accounts of individual suffering. The entire media landscape, online and off, becomes a vast and compelling appeal. All we have to do is show up and ask.

But the media only do this when the human numbers are so big they catch their attention.

Otherwise, we must give every problem an individual face. Not a number.

Most of your donors and prospects already know the problem you're working on is big. The sad thing is that many people don't donate because they think giving is futile. They feel they can't make a difference.

That's our fault. Fundraisers have been hammering away at how big the problems are for so long, many people only know one thing about the world's problems: They're huge. They have no idea we could solve many of our problems if we would get involved.

Let me show you what I mean by fundcrushing:

```
Every year, 15 million hectares of rain-
forest are destroyed. That's more than a
football field of forest every second. Per-
manently gone. With the forest go irreplace-
able plant and animal species. More than
137 species go extinct every day. That's one
every ten minutes.*
```

A donor who reads this message would have to have an iron will to keep caring and stay involved in the cause. It's as if I said to you, "My dog died. Will you donate to save his life?"

If you want to move people to join you in solving this environmental problem, you need to tell a story or paint a

---

* Environmental organizations are often guilty of jaw-dropping feats of fundcrushing. They've made it almost *impossible to care*. In my opinion, the organizations doing this are almost as guilty for the sorry state of the environment as the polluters and exploiters they're fighting.

picture of a solvable piece of it. Give them an opportunity to act heroically and make a difference:

```
The bulldozers are ready. They're parked
on the edge of a patch of tropical forest
that's about the size of the average Ameri-
can backyard. Several dozen gigantic trees
stand waiting too. Each one is up to 200
feet tall, home to birds, reptiles, insects,
mammals—including a very noisy troop of
monkeys.
    It will all be flattened in a matter of
hours. Unless someone like you steps for-
ward with the funds to halt the destruction.
```

A few years ago, *New York Times* columnist Nicholas Kristof wrote about the tepid international response to the humanitarian crisis in Darfur. He cited some now-famous research showing that people were far more charitable when told about a hungry little girl in Africa named Rokia than when told about a deadly famine that threatened millions.

Kristof realized that the reason the Darfur crisis was neglected was because it was *huge*. People *couldn't* care. He theorized there would be more response if Darfur had "a suffering puppy with big eyes and floppy ears."

He was right.

Every fundraising ask must have a puppy! Not necessarily an actual dog but someone whose story tells *the story* in a way that touches the heart. The way a puppy does. If you don't have that, you aren't really fundraising. You're just spreading words around, hoping they'll randomly catch people's attention.

After I read Kristof's piece, I made a sign to remind myself to find the puppy in every fundraising message. Here it is:

Where's the puppy?

You can download this image in color and sized to print on an 8½-by-11-inch sheet at http://is.gd/wheresthepuppy.

Here's how you can change fundcrushing into fundraising:

► Offer bite-size solutions the donor can afford. If you're talking to people likely to give $25, show them what they can accomplish with $25.

► Tell stories about individuals or issues at a scale they can grasp.

▶ Show a clear picture of the solution you want them to be part of.

That's how you win donors' hearts, minds, and donations.

When you slam them with big numbers, you confirm the fear lingering in all our hearts: that we are not significant.

Don't do that to your donors. It's not nice. And it's not fundraising.

CHAPTER 13

Wholehearted Fundraising: Meeting Donors' Emotional Needs

Remember Goofus and Gallant? They're the yin-and-yang brothers who represent the Dark Side of the human heart (Goofus) and the Good Side (Gallant). I met them in the dentist's waiting room of my childhood, which invariably stocked the children's magazine *Highlights*.

Goofus has messy hair and a wicked grin. He's impulsive, rude, and disobedient. Gallant is neatly combed and wears a bland, vacant smile matching his good manners, thoughtfulness, and common sense. Goofus always screws up, but he seems like he'd be fun to hang out with. Gallant does everything right . . . but let's be frank, he's an annoying brownnoser.

Let's imagine Goofus and Gallant grew up to become fundraising copywriters. They'd personify two common approaches:

Goofus bosses his friends.

Gallant asks, "What do you want to do next?"

Goofus and Gallant display two sides of human nature. We can learn a lot from how each of them might approach fundraising. (Copyright Children's Highlights, Inc.)

How Goofus Raises Funds

Goofus tells donors what's *wrong*. He grabs you by the throat, shakes you, and rubs your nose in problems. It doesn't feel good. If you can't or don't want to give, Goofus' approach can leave you feeling guilty.

Goofus fundraising can be harsh, but *it usually works*. After all, donors want to make the world a better place. Starkly pointing out a problem that needs solving is how you stir them to action. Goofus speaks to donors where they are.

Here's how he might raise funds to combat a nasty parasite that plagues some remote areas:

```
It started with a sore bump on Abdul's foot.
Not much more than a pimple. But it kept
getting worse. One night Abdul woke up
screaming. His foot felt like it was on fire.
```

```
His sore, now large and red, had something
that looked like the end of a spaghetti
noodle poking out, twitching back and forth.
He had a guinea worm—a waterborne parasite
that can grow up to four feet long inside
the human body.

    And that meant he now faced about six
weeks of searing pain while a visiting nurse
extracted the worm, twisting it inch by inch
onto a small stick.*
```

There's a downside to Goofus fundraising. It leads to *lower donor retention* over time.

Donors give and they give, responding to the urgency of the appeals, but the problems don't go away. If anything, they seem to get *worse* as Goofus hones his message to an ever-sharper point. You can imagine how that might leave donors feeling hopeless and disengaged . . . and unwilling to give any more.

Low donor retention is the pits. It undermines everything you do in fundraising. Worse yet, it's getting harder (that is, more expensive) to attract new donors to replace those you lose. It's better (cheaper) to keep the donors you have than to find new ones. That's a tall order if the very way you motivate people to give slowly turns them off from giving!

---

* Guinea worm appeals used to be a gold standard challenge for fundraising writers in the international aid sector. So easy to make horrifying. So hard to make believable. It has recently been all but eradicated. That's a great triumph, of course, but I think more than one veteran copywriter looks wistfully back at the rough glory of guinea worm appeals.

How Gallant Raises Funds

Gallant's fundraising is a refreshing contrast. His messages are upbeat and optimistic. He paints beautiful pictures of the positive impact the nonprofit has. He invites donors to be part of the success. It's fundraising the way many organizations want fundraising to be.

Here's how Gallant might tackle the guinea worm appeal:

```
Well-tended fields stretch out in all direc-
tions, dotted with hard-working farmers.
Children shout and laugh while playing soc-
cer outside the well-attended school.

    The village is more prosperous than ever,
thanks in no small part to the fact that
guinea worms no longer exist. People are
working, learning, and playing—not suffer-
ing the painful infestation and aftermath.
```

Gallant fundraising seldom works. The happy stories it tells have *nothing to do with donors*. Instead of telling them what they can do, it's about what the organization has already done. It doesn't present donors with a problem to solve. It may be inspiring for staff, but it's boring for donors. And nobody ever bored anyone into giving. Remember organization-as-hero stories from a few chapters ago? That's Gallant's shtick.

Some claim that what Gallant fundraising lacks in short-term effectiveness is made up in long-term results. Sadly, this isn't true. It's not possible for poor campaign results to somehow add up to good retention. There's no way to keep donors for the long haul if you don't attract them to begin with. That would be like trying to drive across town without pulling out of the driveway.

Organizations using the Gallant approach watch their revenue drop at accelerating rates. Many desperately turn to Goofus tactics to shock their fundraising back to life. When revenue improves, they go back to their old ways. They lurch back and forth between Goofus and Gallant styles in a brand-crushing, schizophrenic dance.

If our only choices were Goofus fundraising or Gallant fundraising, we'd be in a world of hurt, caught between one approach that works in the short term but cuts us off long term, and another that doesn't work at all.

But there's another way.

Wholehearted Fundraising

There's a balanced, realistic, donor-respecting type of fund-raising, and you can easily put it to work. I call it *wholehearted fundraising* because it aligns with the needs of the heart:

- ▶ It gives donors the bad news that spurs them to action.
- ▶ It shows them the good they can accomplish when they give.

At first wholehearted fundraising looks like Goofus fundraising. But it's more. It clearly shows donors that when they give, *progress will be made.* The problem—at least part of it—can be solved. Giving is an act of hope because it works. That's a radical difference from what both Goofus and Gallant do, and it makes a huge difference in fundraising results.

Here's a wholehearted approach to the guinea worm appeal:

```
It started with a sore bump on Abdul's foot.
Not much more than a pimple. But it kept
getting worse. One night Abdul woke up
screaming. His foot felt like it was on fire.
His sore, now large and red, had something
that looked like the end of a spaghetti
noodle poking out of it, twitching back and
forth. He had a guinea worm—a waterborne
parasite that can grow up to four feet long
in the human body.

    It's a horrible situation. But there's a
solution you can make possible. Your gift
today will provide water filters for people
in guinea worm areas. These filters will keep
people from swallowing the microscopic eggs
that grow into guinea worms.
```

Wholehearted fundraising makes the whole thing *about the donor.* How he's needed. What she can do.

Goofus made it about the problem. Gallant made it about the organization. You can make your fundraising about the donor.

Wholehearted fundraising can play on two stages. The first stage is the one I've shown you here: fundraising that displays the problem and solution in the same message.

But wholehearted fundraising truly comes to life when it unfolds over the course of your relationship with the donor. That happens when you develop a cadence across your messages that alternate like this:

- ▶ Hard-hitting asks for funds that point to the solution.
- ▶ Reporting back that proves the donor's gifts really make a difference.*

If your fundraising communications are pummeling your donors with hopeless news like Goofus or lulling them into inaction like Gallant, wholehearted fundraising is the lifeline that can help build an action-oriented relationship with your donors.

---

* Donor-focused newsletters are the main (though not only) place to do this. You can get a Ph.D. in newsletters by reading *Making Money with Donor Newsletters*, by Tom Ahern.

CHAPTER 14

What Good Is Guilt?

It was bad enough that I thought throwing a dirt clod at Kevin would be fun. But I made it worse.

A group of us were throwing rocks down a hillside, aiming at a rusty barrel at the bottom. It made a satisfying clang when you hit it. Good, clean fun. But you know how things can go with boys throwing rocks.

I hurled my rock at Kevin's head. I expected it to burst into a cloud of grit and dust. Instead, it hit him with a hollow thud—a loud sound I can still hear. Kevin toppled over like a tree. Then lay there motionless, blood trickling from above his ear. Half of the kids scattered, yelling. The rest clustered around Kevin. I stood outside the circle, unable to move.

"Dude, you killed him," someone whispered. I knew the awful truth. I had murdered my friend.

Then, a miracle. Kevin sat up. He shook himself, said a four-letter word, and flung a handful of loose dirt at me. Within minutes, he and the others were throwing rocks again.

I didn't recover as quickly. I went behind a tree and vomited. Then walked home on rubbery legs, replaying the scene over and over in my mind, hearing the sound of the rock thunking against his head, seeing him fall.

I still cringe when I think of that day. It changed my life. It made me more careful, less apt to follow an impulse. Even now, if I pick up a rock to throw it, a knot forms in my stomach. I falter. Double-check to make sure there's nobody close by.

Guilt is one of the strongest motivators in human experience. You've no doubt felt its power, too.

But as powerful as it is, guilt is a risky tool for fundraising. There's almost no way to invoke it without creating a backlash that'll put you at odds with donors and cause you to miss the mark.

In fundraising, there are three types of guilt that sometimes show up. Each has its own dangers. Only one is even marginally helpful for motivating donors.

Direct Guilt: The Accusation

```
You haven't done your part to solve the
problem.
```

Some churches used to say this, but you rarely hear it any more. And that's a good thing, because it's toxic.

The main problem is that accusing someone—even someone who fully deserves it—is more likely to make them feel defensive than guilty. The moment they sense an attempt to stir up guilt, they build barriers that destroy the possibility of compassion.

Anyway, a direct accusation in fundraising is misplaced. Donors and prospects aren't the ones who should feel guilty. They're the ones who are involved and doing the right thing.

Indirect Guilt: It's Society's Fault

> Only one in a hundred Americans cares enough about the tragedy in Syria to give even a small donation to ease the suffering!

It's tempting to say something like this, because it seems true. You may think it invokes a type of exclusivity, telling the reader she's one of the special ones. The problem is when you tell donors nobody is giving, you're creating social proof that *not giving* is the norm.

People do what other people do. If you make it clear that others don't give, your message is *Don't give.* You'd be better off telling your donors, *Everyone is giving.*

Implied Guilt: Look at Your Priorities

> For the price of your morning latte, you can save a life.

This is a healthier form of guilt. It's closer to the feeling charitable people actually experience. Donors look at the blessings in their lives. When they consider the needs of others, they can see that giving is clearly the right thing to do.

You may have noticed from reading this book that almost always I advocate being direct. Here's a place where indirect communication works better. To my knowledge, this is the only dependable way for fundraisers to harness the power of guilt. You harness it by not harnessing it.

The truth is some of the gifts you receive are atonement. Careless rock throwing in the distant past and other forms of personal guilt are no doubt part of the motivations of many donors.

The only way to tap into these powerful motivations is to let the donor do the tapping. Other than that, guilt is a terrible fundraising tool you should avoid.

CHAPTER 15

Four Smart Assumptions about Donors

One of the main differences between a professional writer and someone who writes is this: The professional is *obsessed with the audience*. This sometimes confuses non-writers.

They see a writer energetically pursuing information about the audience and think it's a waste of time. "Why don't you just get busy and write?"

Professionals know you won't succeed that way. They know writing that isn't aimed at a specific audience is just word confetti.

Professionals accept that it's our fault when readers don't get our message. If you're playing darts and hit the wall, do you blame the dartboard?

Non-professionals, unaware of the audience, make *themselves* the audience. They write to please and persuade themselves. But as a fundraising writer, you need to become an expert on your donors. You should know their demographics and their psychographics, and have a bank of knowledge about what has succeeded and what has failed to move them.

Not all donor groups are the same. But the following assumptions are common to *most*:

Donors Are Older Than You

If you're eighty-five or older, you can skip this section.

When you write fundraising copy, you're not talking to people like your pals. You're communicating with people like your parents, your aunties, and your grandparents.

Think about the ways you talk with your elderly relatives. Tone, vocabulary, subject matter, allusions—it's different, probably *very* different from your discourse with coworkers and friends.

That's a social adjustment we all make without thinking much about it. But in fundraising you have to be conscious of the difference.

Here are some of the ways writing for older people should play out in fundraising:

- ▶ *Don't be clever.* Cleverness—irony, puns, cool allusions—doesn't cross generational lines well. Be clear and plainspoken. Be so obvious that there's no possible misreading of your message.
- ▶ *Avoid hype.* It's tempting to follow the conventions of commercial advertising because it's well developed and everywhere. But most advertising is aimed at younger audiences. That's why it employs so much hype—big,

bold, exciting claims like *Best! First! Biggest! Newest!* Your donors weren't born yesterday. They know that something claiming to be the greatest ever probably isn't so great. Hype impresses the young and inexperienced.

▶ *Be straightforward.* A lot of advertising relies on symbolism or wordplay to attract attention or make its case. Older people have little patience with these games. Just tell them what's up. They know life is too short to bother with uninteresting riddles.

Donors Are More Emotional Than You

You and I know that the case for giving to your organization is airtight. But most of your excellent facts will *never motivate anyone to give.*

As I've mentioned several times throughout these pages, giving is a deeply emotional act. People give when their hearts tell them to give. Their heads have only the slightest say. When you get down to it, facts are often just noise—resounding gongs or clanging cymbals—in the donor's world.

That's universally true. It's even more pronounced for older people—the majority of your donors. Neuroscience has shown that with age comes a notable shift in brain activity to the right lobe. That's the qualitative, holistic, emotional side. This causes older people to be more emotional in their outlook and more reliant on emotional information. It's a less compartmentalized way of understanding the world. It's also one of the perks of age.

If you're under fifty, you might find it hard to believe that the way a thing feels communicates more than the facts can.

It's true. Trying to persuade someone to give by citing facts is like trying to interest your cat in a nice meal of birdseed. Even premium, top-of-the-line seed isn't interesting to the cat. Give your cat cat food. Give your donors emotional information.

A word picture (or an actual picture) of a child who's crying because she's hungry is more persuasive than a whole battery of facts about world hunger.

Donors Aren't Paying as Much Attention as You Want

There's a gap between you and your donors that's even wider than the age gap. It's the *attention gap.*

You're being *paid* to spend hours every week giving close and critical attention to your fundraising.

By comparison, for donors you're an occasional envelope in a crowded mailbox. One subject line in a long list of emails. A disruptive phone call during dinner. If you're lucky, you have your donor's attention for a few seconds.

It's as if you live in a town for years, studying its climate, geography, and culture, whereas the donor zooms past on the freeway now and then. Sometimes he glances out the window as he passes. If your message isn't completely self-evident in the few seconds of attention you have, it can't get across.

That means one thing: **Keep it simple!**

How simple? Two rules will help:

1. Make only one call to action at a time. If you're asking for money, don't toss in an invitation to your event, or a planned giving offer.

2. Make sure your call to action can be expressed in one sentence. Or less. Save the rain forest. Give a needy child a book. Support Parkinson's research.

Donors *Love* to Give

The other morning on my way to work, a panhandler stepped in front of me. I tried to scoot around but he had me trapped. "I'm really hungry," he said. "I know you got a dollar you can spare. Don't say no."

I had two choices: physically push him out of my way or give him money. I fished a dollar out of my pocket and handed it over. It was the easy way out.

He got his "donation," but I didn't feel good about it. You've probably had similar experiences with telemarketers or door-to-door canvassers. They make you feel lousy, by making you feel trapped into giving.

Your fundraising is not like that—unless you're doing something drastically wrong.

When your donors give, they aren't feeling cornered, they're feeling empowered. They're giving because it expresses their values in action, not just words.

Most donors know the truth that *giving feels good*. You get a quick buzz of pleasure when you give. Then it improves your outlook in general and your whole situation. Charitable giving is one of the secrets to a full, joy-filled life.

So tap into that reality. Create fundraising that assumes donors want to give and are happy to be asked.

Don't write as if you're ashamed of what you're doing and just hoping you aren't doing more damage than absolutely necessary. If you think that way, you're probably making it true.

* * *

On my first day at my first agency-side fundraising job, I was setting up my computer. In those days, a computer was a huge machine that sat on your desk, along with a monitor about the size and weight of a dairy cow.

My monitor had a small photo taped to the upper corner. It was a smiling gray-haired woman. Her slightly awkward pose suggested it was clipped from a church photo directory.

I asked my coworkers about it. They had no idea who the woman was, but as the monitor had belonged to my predecessor, they figured it was his mother or grandmother.

Sometime later I connected with him. My most burning question: *Who is the lady on the monitor?*

"I don't know who she is," he said. "But she stands for my audience. Any time I'm struggling with how to say something I look at the picture and say the words to her. It clears my mind. That photo has saved me countless hours of feeling blocked and frustrated. It's kept me honest, respectful, and relevant."

I kept the photo. It worked for me, too.

Donors are real people—and they aren't you. When you understand that truth, your writing becomes stronger, smarter, and more effective.

PART IV

A Brief Survival Guide

Writing is strange work. Anyone can do it.

That is, any literate person can put words on paper, and some of them, some of the time, can do so with grace and power.

As a professional, you know what it takes to write well. But sometimes someone else—an amateur—has the magic. It's not fair!

I imagine professional basketball players have a similar feeling when a nine-year-old sinks two consecutive free throws from center court during a halftime contest. Everyone in the arena laughs and observes drily to their neighbors, "Our seven-foot center with the multimillion dollar contract can't do that!"

And they aren't wrong, though they're not even close to right. Nobody is considering replacing the seven-foot center with the nine-year-old.

The same thing happens in fundraising.

I've seen salespeople who can hardly compose a coherent email write gripping copy. They understand persuasion, and that by itself can spawn strong writing.

I've seen twenty-four-year-old talented wunderkinds get plum assignments and write miraculous copy.

That's how it is. Anyone can write.

But like the basketball players watching the youngster, we should just shake our heads. We know there's more to greatness than lightning-strike luck. We know careers aren't made on center-court shots. We know it's about showing up. Being mentally ready even when we're sad, tired, or distracted.

One of my favorite descriptions of what it means to be a writer is in the poem "Adam's Curse," by the Irish poet William Butler Yeats:

> A line will take us hours maybe;
> Yet if it does not seem a moment's thought,
> Our stitching and unstitching has been naught.
> Better go down upon your marrow-bones
> And scrub a kitchen pavement, or break stones
> Like an old pauper, in all kinds of weather;
> For to articulate sweet sounds together
> Is to work harder than all these, and yet
> Be thought an idler.

Let's not get carried away. Those who scrub actual kitchen pavements or break real stones work a lot harder than we do. But Yeats captures the laborious nature of writing and the secret that the easier you make it look, the harder you have to work at it.

The final section of this book is about being a writer, specifically a fundraising writer. Among the things we'll explore are:

- ▶ A rule that, if you can put it to work, might lead immediately to far better fundraising results.
- ▶ The enemies who prey on effective fundraising copy and how you can win them over.
- ▶ The traps that lead us astray and how to avoid them.
- ▶ Practical hints for writers from the front lines of the fundraising world.

CHAPTER 16

Who's Ready for the Ahern Rule?

"*This* is why people should give!" the new executive director said. He dramatically threw a newspaper on the table, leaned back, and glowered at everyone sitting around the conference room.

The newspaper was folded open to A13. Near the bottom was a smallish article headlined "Study: Homelessness Up Sharply." It related how there were nearly 20 percent more homeless people in the community than there had been three years before.

"We need to be *straight* with our donors," he continued. "Show them these *facts*—not emotional pabulum."

I was the one who'd cooked up the pabulum.

Specifically, it was a direct mail letter focusing on an unemployed local man who'd lost everything after two years. He was living under a bridge, on a diet of what he called "homeless mac and cheese"—a packet of ramen noodles with a handful of cheese puffs mixed in. The resulting orange stew is warm, fills you up, and tastes almost like real food. But it won't keep you healthy for long.

The executive director *hated* my letter because it zeroed in on one person, not the "real problem" of increasing homelessness. It wasted an entire paragraph on homeless mac and cheese—a meaningless distraction. And my letter never once cited the new study on homelessness. Worse yet, it never mentioned the organization's pioneering program that helped the homeless recover their shattered self-esteem. My letter was about *meals.*

"*Anyone* can serve up meals," the director said. "Our self-esteem program is *unique.*"

In fact, he'd gone to the trouble of composing a letter to replace the travesty I'd written. It was one-page long (mine was four). It opened with an extensive quote from the newspaper, then went on to describe the self-esteem program. Finally it bullet-listed several other programs he was proud of. It didn't directly ask. It just sort of hinted: "Many in our community are banding together against the scourge of homelessness." He didn't want his organization to be known as one that begs for quarters in the street. There was no P.S. ("That's unprofessional," he sniffed.)

You've probably been in a situation like this, so you can guess the outcome. We mailed the executive director's letter, and received the lowest response in the organization's history. It was a devastating loss of revenue, so deep the organization had to let staff go and scale back their services.

The worst thing about my story—you're probably already thinking this—is that *it happens all the time.*

What is it about fundraising that causes people who know nothing about it to feel so confident they can do it better than the pros? People who've never read a fundraising book . . . never read one of the hundreds of blogs on the topic . . . never been to a conference rich with useful content . . . never labored under a mentor who knew the profession—they *know* they can do better than those who've done all that.

Houston, we have a problem. And it's costing us millions, maybe billions, in lost revenue. If Congress were debating a bill that even hinted at doing as much damage to revenue as the misguided red pens do, we'd march on Washington!

How can we stop this!?

There's a solution, and it's already at work: the *Ahern Rule*. It's named after master craftsman Tom Ahern, who has an agreement with his clients: "Unless I've spelled your name wrong, *you don't change my copy*." (He calls it the Verbatim Clause; I'd rather name it after him.)

When Tom writes your fundraising copy, you agree to let him apply his expertise without your guesswork. You have to let him succeed without interference.*

Not every writer is Tom Ahern. Many don't have the mastery to justify a hands-off privilege. And every writer, no matter how talented and experienced, can benefit from the thoughts of someone who knows fundraising and can comment based on facts and experience.

---

* Tom's rule is not quite as set in concrete as it sounds. He happily hears suggestions from his clients, and he freely admits they often make suggestions that strengthen his work. But the rule keeps the garbage out.

But we could raise a lot more money for our causes if we could say, "Thanks for the feedback, but no thanks," to misguided attempts to fix our work.

Someday. Maybe.

CHAPTER 17

Five Fundraising Traps and How to Avoid Them

Sometimes being a writer is like starring in a bad episode of *The Twilight Zone*. You're about to enter a dark forest to do something heroic. An old man appears from nowhere. He fixes you with bloodshot eyes and warns you the forest is full of traps. Traps, everywhere!

He disappears. You scoff and step confidently forward. And fall into a pit.

You scramble out and pitch forward into another. This happens again, and again. So you climb up to the edge of the pit and survey the area. You can't see a single trap anywhere. Just forest floor, carpeted with leaves. You hoist yourself out, take a step, and immediately tumble into another trap.

You sit on the floor of the pit rubbing your bruises. Then the truth hits. The traps aren't in the woods. It's worse than that. The traps are in . . . *your* . . . *mind!*

[Cue creepy music and smug, chain-smoking narrator.]

When you're a writer, the things that trip you up most are inside your head. That's what makes them hard to avoid.

Let's take a survivor's tour of some of the common traps in fundraising writing. I know my way into each one, unfortunately. I also know my way out. Most of the time.

The Trap of Knowledge

There will probably never be a cure for cancer. I know that because I've been involved in cancer fundraising for a long time. Cancer isn't one disease waiting for a cure, but thousands of loosely related, constantly mutating diseases. Some are curable. Others aren't, at least not yet, but they're treatable. Big picture, the news is *very* good.

Asking a donor to help fund the "cure for cancer" is misleading.

But giving donors a lecture on the non-curability of cancer (like the one I just gave) is exactly the wrong message in fundraising. Doing so is a sign you've fallen into the Trap of Knowledge.

Your knowledge can create a wall separating you from donors. It keeps you from thinking and talking as they do. It encourages you to badger those who know less than you—that is, almost everyone.

Your knowledge is also the tool you'll use to escape the Trap of Knowledge.

Let's say you want donors to join you in the fight against cancer. A basic, bare-bones call to action might read like this:

```
Please send your gift to help find the cure
for cancer.
```

If supported with an emotional story and specific reasons to give, this could be effective.

But if you've fallen into the Trap of Knowledge, you might find yourself unable to say something so simple. You'd want to revise the statement by watering down the cure for cancer premise:

```
There will never be a cure for cancer. But
we are advancing on multiple fronts, with
new treatments and promising avenues open-
ing all the time. Please join us.
```

Not inspiring! (And telling donors what we and they *can't do* is terrible fundraising.) It would be better to *change the premise.* Make a simpler statement. Talk about something that *is happening*:

```
The end of cancer as we know it is coming.
Soon! Every dollar you give gets us closer
to the day when cancer will no longer take
our loved ones. Join the fight now!
```

That doesn't raise the red-herring issue of the cure, but gives the donor something exciting she can become part of.

Every cause has its own world of complexity. There are people in your organization who live and breathe that complexity. Not you. As a writer, you must be a master of simplicity. Clarity in the form of battle cries that will rally donors.

The Trap of the Wrong Audience

Donors can be a faceless crowd that's hard to understand. They give fuzzy, indirect—and in the case of direct mail, long-delayed—feedback on your writing.

When you don't have a direct connection with your audience, you might aim at a group that's closer: your colleagues. They're smart and likable. Most important, they're present. They can give you detailed critiques on how fundraising ought to be. They can be articulate and persuasive about that.

And wrong.

They aren't wrong about what they want. But they're wrong—astonishingly wrong—on what motivates donors to give.

    What your colleagues find
    motivating will not work for
    donors.

I made that large because it's so important: *Your colleagues don't get it.*

They're a fine group. They're just the wrong audience. What they prefer is wrong. Not randomly wrong, but diametrically and automatically wrong.

Your colleagues aren't the only wrong audience. Your spouse, your kids, the bartender, your friends—they'll all lead you astray, too. Even your mom, who could be a perfect demographic match with your donors, will give you bad information. That's because every person's *conscious* opinion of how they *would* respond to fundraising has nothing to do with reality. We simply don't know how we would respond. So we guess. And we guess wrong.

Here are some ways to help you focus on your real audience:

1. *Be obsessive about what works.* Learn everything you can. Test as often as possible. Fundraising results are the ultimate reality check. They can be puzzling, but they'll never give you bad advice.

2. *Find ways to talk with donors.* Not your pals who happen to be donors, but typical donors. Spend time in your call center. Attend events that attract donors. Even focus groups can give insight into the surprising ways donors think about your cause.

3. *Focus on one person.* Have in your mind a specific person who stands for your donor (like the photo on the monitor in chapter 15). Address your fundraising messages to her. Imagine the questions she'd ask and answer them. Cultivate a sense of what might confuse her and what motivates her. This mental exercise will make it easier to discover the right tone for your messages.

The Trap of Numbers

We talked about this trap back in chapter 12. I'm bringing it up again because so many fundraisers fall into it. The facts—the amazing numbers about our causes—are such a temptation. The shocking number of children who die from hunger every day. The millions of people diagnosed with serious diseases each year. The breathless speed of deforestation.

Facts like these seem compelling to you and me. But they can lead us into the Trap of Numbers. We think that because a problem is big, it's motivating. But what works in fundraising is the exact opposite. People don't give because the problem is big. *They give because it's solvable.* That is, a *small problem* is more compelling than a big one.

When you tell donors a problem is gigantic, you're warning them *away from giving.* You're using secret brain language to say, *Forget it. This is not something you can deal with.*

The Trap of Cleverness

You're intelligent. You love words. You have an active mind, and possibly a slight allergy to the same old same old.

Look out! It's a trap!

The Trap of Cleverness gets us when we let ourselves get bored with our work.

It's not just us fundraisers. Cleverness is epidemic in journalism and advertising. Clever, punny headlines turn reading some newspapers into a frustrating lost-in-the-funhouse exercise. And we've all seen advertisements that think they can sell perfume by showing a wineglass shattering in slow motion, because that's a metaphor for something or other.

The cleverness epidemic is brought to you by people who are bored with being clear and literal. They also may have discovered that it's beyond their skills to be plainspoken and exciting at the same time (even though that's the job description of every writer whose goal is persuasion or motivation).

Avoid these types of cleverness in your fundraising:

- ▶ *Wordplay.* Hardly anyone else enjoys puns and word tricks the way you and I do. If your fundraising pitch to upgrade an old building and rid it of dangerous materials has a headline like *We're Doing Asbestos We Can*, you're being clever, not communicating, and certainly not fundraising.
- ▶ *Symbolism.* Always tell your donors literally what they need to know. Don't resort to symbolic ways even when that might be beautiful. There's a video produced by a nonprofit in which every time villagers in India get help, they start floating three feet above the ground. Because, y'know, helping them lifts them. That organization found it more interesting to show people floating than to reveal their actual problems and the real, reachable solutions donors could make possible.
- ▶ *Abstraction.* Donors want to do specific things to change the world. They're far more likely to feed hungry children than fight poverty. They'd rather keep the opera going than support the arts. And they'd rather do almost anything than stand up for an abstraction like *Hope*.

Ultimately, cleverness doesn't work in fundraising because it's about *you*, not your donors. It's the technique of self-centered show-offs, not people who raise funds and connect donors with causes they care about.*

The Trap of Good News

The most frequently repeated poor fundraising advice goes like this: *Show people how effective and successful our programs are. That will encourage them to give. Everyone likes to be part of success!*

It's true we'd rather be part of success than failure. But when your message tells success stories and omits *need* or the situation you want donors to help change, you skip the main step that moves donors to action.

Donors give to solve problems. They give to save, to rescue, to defend. To turn bad situations good. They're rarely motivated to maintain a desirable status quo. Telling donors you've already taken care of the problem tells them they aren't needed.

Most people in your organization would prefer that your fundraising focus on good news. It makes them feel better. But it's not effective fundraising. (Remember wholehearted fundraising back in chapter 14?)

* * *

You are most safe from the errors that undermine your writing when you've recently escaped the traps that caused

---

* I periodically post critiques of "clever" nonprofit messages. You can see them at http://is.gd/stupidnonprofitads.

you to go astray—when you remember what it was like to be trapped and confused.

Likewise, you're most in danger when you forget. When it seems like there are no traps to worry about, and everything you do feels smart and on target.

Keep your eyes open. The traps are in front of you, and you can fall in at any time.

CHAPTER 18

Things I Wish I'd Learned Sooner

I love the effortless mastery of carpenters. The way they pound a nail with five swift blows—perfectly straight, exactly in place, no smashed fingers, no circular scars in the wood.

Carpenters don't think it's amazing. That's just how it goes when you get a lot of practice and work around other carpenters.

Every profession has a body of knowledge and a set of skills that are passed along person to person. With respect to fundraising, I offer the following:

Your First Draft Is Bad

I don't have to read your stuff. I already know. Your first draft is dreadful. So is mine. And every other writer's. That's the nature of first drafts.

Knowing this, being comfortable with it, is one of the marks of a professional.

The professional doesn't waste time and energy trying to save sentences and phrases that went into the first draft. He just goes to work obliterating the garbage and getting to the gem that's hidden there.

Let yourself write a bad first draft. It's going to be bad no matter what you do, so go for it.

This will also free you from writer's block, which is mostly fear of being bad. Once you know you'll be back again to fix the mess, you can make progress and not get bogged down by fear or the delusion that you must get everything right the first time.

To keep moving, I used to type the word *lobster* whenever I hit a wall and couldn't think of something good. That freed me to move on. It also forced me to come back later and deal with it. After all, I didn't want to hand in copy with passages like this:

```
Would you please help lobster lobster
lobster.
```

I've since discovered it's just as effective, and quicker, to pound out random letters. Try it. It'll make you a happier, less anxious writer. And get you more quickly beyond that terrible first draft.

Get Rid of the First Few Paragraphs

Even after you've whipped your copy into shape, there's still part of your piece that's not up to standard: *the beginning.*

I've reviewed thousands of direct mail fundraising letters, emails, and other projects. Almost every time—and I'm talking about the work of skilled professional writers—the writing is improved by axing the beginning, anywhere from the first sentence to the first few paragraphs. This includes my own writing. It's so consistently true I could cut the beginning without even reading it, and I'd usually improve the piece.

Cutting the first few paragraphs can be painful because most of us work harder on the beginning than on the rest of the piece. But here's the weird thing. That hard work isn't real writing. It's warm-up.

Warm-up is important. Some part of your mind knows that, which is why you do it—just as an athlete does. But your warm-up is even less interesting than his. Don't make your donors read your warm-up. It's a waste of their time and more likely to confuse them than move them to action.

Have a Swipe File and Use It

Every fundraising writer should have a swipe file: a box full of direct mail fundraising and a huge in-box of saved email. Without this, you're half the fundraiser you could be.

You need to know what's happening in the field. You also need material. Let me be clear: When I say use your swipe file, I mean *steal from it*. Any time you're stuck, blocked, or just in need of a quick start, pick something interesting from the swipe file and start adapting it to your needs. Don't worry about plagiarism; by the time you're finished, there will be nothing left of the original.

You'll also find a lot of cautionary material. Let's face it. There's a lot of bad, sloppy fundraising in our donors' mailboxes. You might be surprised how inspiring bad fundraising can be. It has spurred me to some of my best work. *Don't do what this poor sap did*, I think, and proceed with renewed energy and focus.

Here's how to build a great swipe file:

► Get on as many nonprofit lists as you can. (This may require you to donate; more on that shortly.)

► Ask everyone—coworkers, family, friends—to give you their unopened fundraising mail. They'll think you're a weirdo, but they'll enjoy helping you.

► Find at least one older friend or relative who receives a lot of direct mail and ask her to save everything for you.*

Believe in Magic, but Don't Count on It

The best ideas you'll come up with will appear out of thin air. You'll be shaving, painting the kitchen, or stuck in traffic, and suddenly the solution to a problem you were struggling with will pop into your head.

---

* My best source is my Uncle Maynard, who gets a prodigious amount of direct mail. I post on my blog discoveries from Uncle Maynard's mail. You can see them at http://is.gd/unclemaynard.

Freewriting

F reewriting is to writing what exercise is to your physical health. It's a way to condition and strengthen your writing "muscle."

Here's how you do it:

- Set a timer for 10 minutes.
- Start writing. Don't stop to think or read what you've written until time is up. Just write.
- Ignore grammar, spelling, and punctuation. Nobody else needs to read what you write. It's okay if you write garbage.
- If you don't have any ideas, write anyway. If you don't have anything to say, write nonsense. If all you can think of is how annoying this exercise is, just write *I hate freewriting*. If you feel bored or uncomfortable, write about that.

That's it. Do it every day. You will get better at writing.

You might be surprised how often you solve a writing problem you've been struggling with during freewriting. But that's not the point. The point is exercise, and you get that even if you only write garbage, day after day.

Take my word for it, freewriting will make you a stronger, happier, more fluent, more effective writer.

Or you'll bang out a huge project in a fraction of the time it should take—and it's *good*. It's as if you temporarily worked at double speed like a video on fast-forward.

These things happen. They feel like miracles. Perhaps they are. If you believe in the magic, you'll experience it more often.

But the magic isn't on call.

So you have to approach every project as if there will be *no magic*, because that's how it usually is.

Donate

Imagine a music critic who hates music. A sports journalist bored by sports. A science writer who thinks science is bunk.

We pity such people. How can they live such empty, defeated lives? They suck the joy out of their fields. They infect others with their cynicism and sadness.

Fundraisers who aren't donors are like that. They don't get it. They can't get it. The very best advice I have for fundraising writers is this: donate.

When you're a donor, you join the community. You're not a carpetbagger coming from outside to exploit. You're part of the action.

Donating will give you gut insight into the world of your donors. You'll understand for yourself things like:

> ▶ *Giving feels good.* This is simple brain chemistry. It also hooks you to something deeper, something transcendent that enriches your life.

▶ *Being asked rarely hurts.* It's an honor and a source of joy. It's only annoying when it's irrelevant and out of touch with your life. As a donor, you'll be better able to see the difference between what's good and what's irrelevant.

▶ *Giving makes your life better.* It literally improves your mental health, your outlook, and your physical health. It improves self-esteem and makes you feel more in control in our chaotic world. Studies show that it even improves your financial situation.

What I'm saying here may seem strange, and not too credible if you aren't a donor. But if you are, you get it. And that opens the doors to your greatest work.

*   *   *

Back in the introduction to this book, I referred to writers as the Marines of fundraising. I don't mean that lightly.

I've had the privilege of working on Marine Corps–related fundraising, so I've learned a few things about them. One is a key concept the Marines call *force multiplier.*

The Marines get the rough jobs. They're also last in line for funding and equipment. That's why they rely on force multipliers—things that increase their impact from within. Other fighting forces boost their power by adding more people or using better equipment. The Marines can do it without these things.

Their most important force multiplier is their culture. Every Marine knows it. The history they're part of, the mental toughness they train for, the group cohesion expressed in their slogan *Semper fi*—always faithful. The culture makes a difference. A measurable, dependable difference.

Something like it is available to you as a fundraising writer. A spirit, a sense of who you are and what your job is, a mental agility non-writers don't quite get.

We don't have a training and indoctrination program like the Marines. In fact, we're as ragtag and disjointed a group as you can imagine.

Writing, by its nature, can be an isolated and isolating job. Further, if you're like most, you're the only writer in your organization. But don't let these things cut you off from your corps! *Don't go it alone.*

Participate in your profession. Find other fundraising writers to hang out with—online or in the real world. Attend conferences. Read books. Follow blogs. These ordinary acts can transform your professional life.

Most of all find your force multiplier by cultivating a quiet pride in what you do. Against all odds, your work *powers philanthropy.*

Your cause may be hard to describe, harder yet to make exciting. You may have a boss who wants you to do it wrong. You may be underfunded and understaffed. And for certain, your donors are changing their attitudes and preferences—with no fair warning to help you meet their needs.

But you're handling it anyway. You are a stalwart, a professional, a wonder-worker. You are a member of a special tribe—the writers who power the funding of the great causes of our world.

Acknowledgments

No writing task is done solo. Least of all one that's about writing. The only reason I have anything to say about this subject is because I work with other fundraising writers. To each of them I owe a personal and professional debt and thanks for constructing the foundation this book is built on.

First, my colleague writers at TrueSense Marketing. Thanks for being superb and for challenging me every day: George Crankovic, Maria Harmer, Alan Hyams, Everett Lowe, Jolene Miklas, Jennifer Miller, Sarah Onofrey, Andrew Rogers, and Macklin White.

Thanks also to the many other exceptional writers I've been privileged to work with throughout my career, including Bob Ball, Richard DeVeau, Seth La Tour, Peter Li, John McWhinney, Julie Mills, Bruce Ortman, Jill Perry, Kris Poggioli, Joey Scanapico, and Steven Screen.

Of the industry leaders and authors who have created and shepherded our profession, I especially want to thank two: Tom Ahern, who has generously read my manuscripts and encouraged me—and who brings a new sense of fun to the work; and the pioneer Roger Craver, whom I imagine standing there with the stone tablets as the rest of us in the fundraising industry look up sheepishly from our golden-calf distractions.

And finally, thanks to Bob Screen, my first real mentor.

About the Author

Jeff Brooks has been writing for and about nonprofit fundraising for more than 25 years. A propagandist for the donor-focused fundraising revolution, he blogs at www.futurefundraisingnow.com and podcasts at www.fundraisingisbeautiful.com.

His previous books are *The Fundraiser's Guide to Irresistible Communications*, *The Money-Raising Nonprofit Brand*, and an unpublished novel about a man who smuggles plastic consumer goods out of the United States.

He lives in Seattle between an elementary school and a cemetery.

America's All-Time Bestselling Fundraising Books for Securing Major Gifts

Fund Raising Realities Every Board Member Must Face
A 1-Hour Crash Course on Raising Major Gifts for Nonprofit Organizations

David Lansdowne

From the first page, you and your board will be hooked on this one-hour-to-read gem.

The warmth, encouragement, the finely tuned examples and easy readability make for an inviting package that draws you in at once.

Without wasting a word, Lansdowne distills the essence of big-gifts fundraising into 43 "realities" and explains each principle and technique in a way board members will understand instantly.

Put this classic in your board's hands, in their orientation packet, in their annual meeting folder, in their workshop handouts. Put it anywhere you need the art of fundraising illuminated in a masterful, uncomplicated, and engaging way.

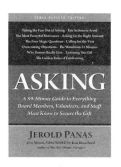

ASKING
A 59-Minute Guide to Everything Board Members, Volunteers, and Staff Must Know to Secure the Gift

Jerold Panas

It ranks right up there with public speaking. Nearly all of us fear it. And yet it's critical to the success of our organizations. Asking for money. It makes even the stout-hearted quiver. But now comes a book, *Asking,* and short of a medical elixir, it's the next best thing for emboldening board members, volunteers, and staff to ask with skill, finesse … and powerful results.

Asking convincingly shows that it doesn't take stellar sales skills to be an effective asker. Nearly everyone can be successful if they follow Panas' step-by-step guidelines.

Emerson & Church, Publishers
www.emersonandchurch.com

Copies of this and other books from the publisher are available at
discount when purchased in quantity for boards of directors or staff.
Call 508-359-0019 or visit www.emersonandchurch.com

Emerson
& Church
PUBLISHERS

15 Brook Street • Medfield, MA 02052
Tel. 508-359-0019 • Fax 508-359-2703
www.emersonandchurch.com